Praise for

SILVER SCREEN FIEND

"Patton Oswalt is one of the most brilliant comedy minds of a generation. This book confirms it."

—Ricky Gervais

"I loved this book. It feels like a great one-sided conversation from your funniest friend. It made me feel less alone in the precious hours I read it. But now it's gone and I have nothing."

—Amy Schumer

"*Silver Screen Fiend* is both a love letter to artistic obsession and a string of caution tape around it. Patton describes the ecstatic demands of the arts (in this case, stand-up and film) with insight, fond pity, and unfailing humor. This is a book for anyone who strives to be great, or is bored in an airport."

—Joss Whedon

"Smart and pointed. [Oswalt] is a colorful writer."

—NPR

"A funny and sentimental read . . . deep, passionate, and personal."

—*The Daily Beast*

"Immediate and vital . . . [*Silver Screen Fiend* is] enough to make any reader seek out the many films that made him hibernate in the first place."

—*The A.V. Club*

"Oswalt's prose is sparkling. . . . A coming-of middle-age meditation, Oswalt's homage to films is both hilarious and heartfelt."

—*USA Today*

"Oswalt is . . . a formidable storyteller. . . . A love song to the silver screen."

—*Paste*

"Vivid and funny."

—*Entertainment Weekly*

"[Oswalt has] a set of synapses like a pinball machine and a prose style to match. . . . Oswalt's writing gives off the hallucinogenic shimmer of the true obsessive, packing all the sharpness and bite of his stand-up."

—*The New York Times*

"Clever and readable . . . Oswalt's encyclopedic knowledge and frothing enthusiasm for films (from sleek noir classics, to gory B movies, to cliche-riddled independents, to big empty blockbusters) is relentlessly present, whirring in the background like a projector."

—*The Boston Globe*

"Oswalt is a great conveyer of his real-life (and reel-life) experiences . . . great insider stuff."

—*The Plain Dealer*

"Entertaining and maniacally informative."

—*Tampa Bay Times*

"[An] astute, acerbic, and footnote-crazy chronicle of life as a 'movie freak mole man.' . . . Oswalt is a true cinephiliac, equally appreciative of the artistry of Jean Cocteau's *Beauty and the Beast* and Doris Wishman's *Bad Girls Go to Hell*."

—*The Philadelphia Inquirer*

"Anyone who loves movies . . . will be better for reading this enjoyable and funny memoir."

—*The Columbus Dispatch*

"A must for fans of comedy and film."

—*Ithaca.com*

Also by Patton Oswalt

Zombie Spaceship Wasteland

SILVER
SCREEN FIEND

． ｡ ｡ ｡ ｡ ｡ ｡

LEARNING ABOUT LIFE
FROM AN ADDICTION TO FILM

PATTON OSWALT

SCRIBNER

New York   London   Toronto   Sydney   New Delhi

SCRIBNER
A Division of Simon & Schuster, Inc.
1230 Avenue of the Americas
New York, NY 10020

First Scribner trade paperback edition October 2015

SCRIBNER and design are registered trademarks of The Gale Group, Inc.,
used under license by Simon & Schuster, Inc., the publisher of this work.

For information about special discounts for bulk purchases,
please contact Simon & Schuster Special Sales at 1-866-506-1949
or business@simonandschuster.com.

The Simon & Schuster Speakers Bureau can bring authors to your live event.
For more information or to book an event, contact the Simon & Schuster
Speakers Bureau at 1-866-248-3049 or visit our website at
www.simonspeakers.com.

Interior design by Erich Hobbing

Manufactured in the United States of America

3   5   7   9   10   8   6   4   2

Library of Congress Control Number: 2014017626

ISBN 978-1-4516-7321-0
ISBN 978-1-4516-7322-7 (pbk)
ISBN 978-1-4516-7323-4 (ebook)

Portions of this edition's "Collected Writings on Film" previously
appeared in *Ain't It Cool News*, *Popcorn Fiction*, and *The Dissolve*.

For Sherman Torgan,
all twenty-four frames of this
are yours

"Film is a disease, when it infects your bloodstream, it takes over as the number one hormone . . . it plays Iago to your psyche. As with heroin, the antidote to film is more film."

—Frank Capra

"Oh Bert, do stop this worrying. You must have heard surely of 'movie magic.' You should be a stunt man, who is an actor, who is a character in a movie, who is an enemy soldier. Who'll look for you amongst all those? People like to believe in things, and policemen are just people. Or so I'm told. Frankly, our problem is so simple it's almost beneath us. Now listen to me: That door is the looking glass, and inside it is Wonderland. Have faith Alice! Close your eyes and enjoy."

—Peter O'Toole, in Richard Rush's *The Stunt Man*

"Already the present starts plotting its recurrence
    somewhere in the future, weaving what happens
in among our fabrics, launching its aroma, its music
    imbuing itself into floorboards, plaster, nothing can
stop it, it can't stop itself. You will never have access
    to its entirety, and you have asked how to calculate
what resists calculation . . ."

—Timothy Donnelly, "Dream of the Overlook"

"This WAS our dream, surrounding us. The fucking studios! People's dreams were their business, and they knew their business. They had us by the heart, and we just walked, and looked around, and longed, all the way to the cattle chutes."

—Michael Shea, *The Extra*

"No good movie is too long and no bad movie is short enough."

—Roger Ebert

Contents

CONTENTS

CONTENTS

SILVER SCREEN FIEND

I like to drink.
At my drunkest the worst I do is rewatch
Murder on the Orient Express or fall asleep.
I used to smoke a lot of pot. All it made me do
was go on long walks by myself and laugh at things.
I've enjoyed my share of LSD and mushrooms.
They exploded my being from the inside out—
while I sat and listened to music.

I've done my due diligence as far as vices,
but I'm an unbearable slouch when it comes
to interesting stories connected to them.

This will be either the most interesting or
the most boring addiction memoir you've ever read.
I can't promise it ever gets "harrowing,"
but I can promise that I tried—I really tried—
to make it funny.

Here we go.

CHAPTER ONE

Movie Freaks
and Sprocket Fiends

The New Beverly Cinema,
May 20, 1995

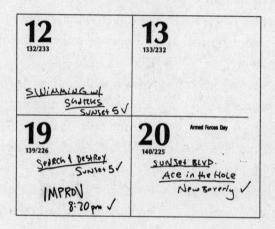

Listen—you don't *have* to follow me into the darkness here. It's sunny out. It's a syrupy Los Angeles Saturday afternoon in May of 1995. We're standing on Beverly Boulevard, just west of La Brea. Wide, pleasant street. A few blocks' walk from restaurants, some vintage furniture stores, coffee. Midnineties hipsters are wearing what they think is cool that week. Orthodox Jews committed to their wardrobe thousands of years ago and are walking it like they talk it. Life's going on.

We're about to enter the New Beverly Cinema for a double feature of Billy Wilder's 1950 smash-hit, critically acclaimed *Sunset Boulevard*. Wilder cowrote and directed *Sunset Boulevard* in 1950, took home an Oscar for alchemizing its brilliance at the typewriter, and saw it nominated for ten more Oscars. Wilder etched his name onto the first year of a new decade with a knife made of ink and celluloid.

I can see you want to say something here but now the Fact Fever is on me, and I bulldoze right over you and keep gabbing.

The second feature on the double bill is *Ace in the Hole*, Wilder's follow-up. Cowritten and directed, again, by Wilder. A man who had not only *Sunset Boulevard* behind him but also *Double Indemnity* and *The Lost Weekend*. He wasn't simply "riding a wave of success" when he started *Ace in the Hole*. He was on a three-engine speedboat of triumph and he punched *through* the waves like a shark gone blood simple on surfer guts. He pushed his winnings back onto a single square at the roulette wheel of cinema and gave it a confident spin.

Wait, let me finish. I know, hang on . . .

Where was I? Oh yeah—*Ace in the Hole. That one.* The opposite of *Sunset Boulevard*, success-wise. Double zeroes. House wins. Box office bomb, critical revulsion. Some cynical industry types nicknamed the movie *Ass in the Wringer.* Poor Wilder got one Oscar nomination for Best Screenplay (back when the writing category for

Oscars was divided up between Motion Picture Story and Screenplay) and saw Jan Sterling, the lead actress, grab a much-deserved National Board of Review for her sly, reptilian tour de force. The Venice Film Festival tossed an International Award into his bruised, bloodied lap, as well as nominating him for a Golden Lion (which he lost).

Not that the awards stopped there. In 2007—*fifty-six years later*—*Ace in the Hole* was nominated for a Satellite Award for Best Classic DVD. Which it lost to the fortieth-anniversary edition of *The Graduate*.

Hang. On. In a minute. *Sheesh.*

Billy Wilder still had *Stalag 17*, *Sabrina*, *The Seven Year Itch*, *Some Like It Hot* and *The Apartment* ahead of him. At the bottom of this particular valley in his career was a trampoline, apparently.

I could go on, and I do. This is where you start to pull away. Where you *should* start to pull away. Even though you're talking to a relatively fresh-faced twenty-six-year-old on a sunny sidewalk, you can tell something's wrong, can't you? The way I talk in unwieldy chunks of paragraphs, rather than inquisitive sentences. I'm a boxing glove with a horseshoe inside of it, conversationally. I speak at you. I speak *through* you. You've got the queasy feeling you might not even need to *be* here right now, and I'd still spit Facts About Billy Wilder into the afternoon air.

You're not up for two movies? Hmmm. Wanna just see the one? I mean, you've gotta see *Sunset Boulevard*. *Gotta.* You've never seen it? How can you be alive and not have seen *Sunset Boulevard*?* I mean, I'm definitely seeing both of these, but if you only want to catch *Sunset Boulevard* and then split, fine with me. There are cameos by Erich von Stroheim and Buster Keaton, and did you know that Jack Webb is . . . ?

. . . Really? You're gonna bail?

That's cool. Maybe I'll call you later.

I turn to the ticket booth and hand my $5 to Sherman Torgan, the owner and visionary behind the New Beverly. This is my first time, ever, visiting the theater. Sherman stares from the scratched, grimy ticket booth window. White coals glowing under gray glass, those eyes. I've sat in booths like that before, taking tickets, with zero interest in the customers handing their money through. I stared out at a procession of faces, most of them tilted up and away from me, at the different choices playing at the multiplex I once worked at. The New Beverly has one screen, and Sherman's customers know what's playing. And they rarely tilt their heads up. Their eyes are, more often than not, aimed at the ground. Or, like mine, into the middle distance.

Sherman takes my money and hands me two pale,

---

*This same conversation is happening, simultaneously, across every other facet of the arts. It's happened before I say this to you, it's happening while I say this to you and it will keep on happening, forever and ever. Someone at a used record store is admonishing a friend for never having heard Love's *Forever Changes*. At a used bookstore, an ever-ravenous bookworm shakes their head sadly at their friend, who's never read Charles Portis's *Masters of Atlantis*. Or someone's never had the fries at the Apple Pan. Or encountered Michael C. McMillen's art installation *The Central Meridian*. Or visited Joshua Tree. An infinite crowd of apostles, spreading the word to their unwashed, heathen acquaintances.

orange tickets. There's no one to tear them when I enter, passing to his right and crossing the six or seven feet of dingy carpet to the concession stand, where the air becomes saltier, greasier, stickier and all-around more delicious as I approach. I weigh the cost of a medium popcorn against a large one. In the booth, Sherman files away the memory of my face. He remembers everyone, I'm soon to discover. In four years, to the *exact day* I've purchased the ticket that's now in my pocket, I'll find out exactly how sharp Sherman's memory is.

But now it's 1995, and the first of many nourishing, sun-warmed days has been pushed behind me, behind the swinging doors of the New Beverly. I take my bent, warped-spring seat in the briny darkness. This is the sort of abyssal darkness deep-sea fishes thrive on. Fueling themselves on glowing, volcanic vents on the ocean floor. The New Beverly has a volcanic vent of its own—up on the wall, there, big enough for a *megalodon* shark to swim through. Or a horde of zombies to shuffle through. Or a fleet of spaceships to fly through. Or a teardrop on Ingrid Bergman's hopeful, heartbroken face to slip through. Me and the other deep-sea fishes inside the New Beverly—the movie freaks, sprocket fiends,* celluloid junkies, single-

---

*Sprocket fiend is the name I have for the subterranean dimension to my film addiction. The subtle, beneath-the-sound-track sound of the clattering projector in those old rep theaters, *especially* the New Beverly. The defiant, twenty-four-frames-per-second mechanical heartbeat that says, at least for the duration of whatever movie you're watching, the world's time doesn't apply to you. You're safe in whatever chronal flow the director chooses to take you through. Real time, or a span of months or years, or backward and forward through a life. You are given the space of a film *to steal time*. And the projector

star satellites and garden-variety misanthropes, loners and sun haters—we, too, feed from the glow pulsing off of the screen. The movie screen—*that's* our volcanic vent.

Trailers for upcoming movies unspool—*The Nutty Professor* is playing on Tuesday, along with *Cinderfella*. Hmm. *Repulsion* and *Knife in the Water.* Never seen either at this point in my life. Gonna check those off. It's starting to dawn on me, as I sit in the New Beverly and munch, alternately, popcorn (salt) and Red Vines (sweet), that this is the beginning of My Training. My Training to Become a Great Filmmaker. Hasn't Scorsese seen every movie ever made, and doesn't he still lurk in his Manhattan loft, projecting some obscure British horror movie on a 16 mm projector, looking to be inspired by a single out-of-context tableaux of brilliance? The summer before now I was disintegrated and reassembled by Quentin Tarantino's *Pulp Fiction* at the Alhambra in San Francisco. Isn't Tarantino this holy fool who can take various parts of disintegrated movies and reassemble them into a greater whole? Like . . . like . . . oh! Yeah! Like that scene in *The Good, the Bad and the Ugly*, where Eli Wallach disassembles all of the different revolvers to make the Supergun he's going to use to ventilate Clint Eastwood? *There*! Haven't I done, *just now* with the Eli Wallach analogy, what Tarantino does on a more epic, transcendent scale in his films?

I remember walking out of that screening a year before, when *Pulp Fiction* had finished its Möbius-strip narra-

---

is your only clock. And the need for that subtle, clicking sprocket time makes you—made me—a sprocket fiend.

tive and the audience floated back out into the world on the magic carpet of Dick Dale's "Miserlou." I saw it with Blaine Capatch and Marc Maron, two comedian friends.*

"You wanna go get some lunch, or some coffee?" asked Blaine.

I said, "Nah, I gotta go."

"Where?" snapped Maron. "Gotta go home and burn that screenplay you were working on?"

Good one, Marc. And good advice, as it turned out. I hadn't even considered writing screenplays up to that point. My ambition then—six years into a stand-up career—was to get an HBO special. The rest of my Career Whiteboard was a blue question mark in erasable ink.

And here I am, a year later. Sitting down to devour two Billy Wilder films. One I've seen (*Sunset*) one I haven't (*Ace*). A fledgling completist. It starts here. And on an *actual movie screen*, so I can clock the experience of how I react to the film. As well as the unspoken vibe of the audience around me, of how the amorphous, mass "we" responds to the film. What pierces us. What pings off us, leaving only an echo. What passes through us. What misses us. Look at me—aren't I a diligent soon-to-be filmmaker, doing my time in the darkness like this? Not just watching movies on videotapes or, someday if I ever get rich, DVDs? On. A. Screen. This is a serious crossroads in my life, a new path, and I'm confidently making my first steps.

By sitting in the dark.

No, I'm no dilettante. Light through celluloid, onto a

---

*Well, Maron was—and still is—a beloved frenemy.

movie screen. Darkness and uncomfortable seats. That's the only way I'll see these, from now on. Give me more laps, coach. I'm a champion. Someday. Can't you see it?

More trailers. *Touch of Evil* and *Kiss of Death* are coming up. Noir! *Nice!* I became addicted to film noir during the three years I lived in San Francisco, when the Roxie Theater on Sixteenth Street would do its noir festival every spring. I saw H. Bruce Humberstone's brilliant *I Wake Up Screaming* in 1993. That scene where psycho policeman Laird Cregar* stares, openmouthed and turtle-eyed, as the film of his now-dead, unattainable dream girl plays in the smoky interrogation room? The one he's using to torment slick, grinning Victor Mature, hoping to railroad the poor bastard into the electric chair?

That got me. Wow, did that get me. It was Franken-stein's monster staring at his hissing, stitched-together Bride and knowing she'd never return his truehearted, cemetery love. It was also me—although I didn't know it yet—shoveling popcorn and licorice into my gaping mouth while every film I would devour off of the New Beverly's stained screen could march and lunge and glide and swoop out of the darkness. *I'll create one of those someday*, I tell myself. *And my films will march and lunge and glide and swoop in ways no one has ever dreamed of. All I have to do is keep watching. I'll know when to make my move.*

At this point in my life, I have every reason to believe

---

*Died young. Thirty-one. Heart attack after a crash diet. He had the girth and skull of an unforgettable character actor, but he tried to whittle himself into a boring leading man. The knife hit bone.

that this is a viable process for mastering a creative skill. This strategy worked for me before. For instance: When I was nineteen, I wanted to be a comedian. I'd spent the first nineteen years of life memorizing every comedy album I could play on my parents' turntable. I knew the exact timing for the pause between the words *waited* and *July* in Bill Cosby's "Revenge" routine.* Not only did I memorize every heckler put-down on Rodney Dangerfield's *No Respect* and Steve Martin's *A Wild and Crazy Guy*, I could even recite, perfectly, the hecklers—walking themselves into vinyl, drunken, douchebag immortality. Yes, I could recite George Carlin's "seven dirty words" and all of their permutations, Richard Pryor's multicharacter "God Was a Junkie" off of *Supernigger* and pretty much every single flawless word from Emo Philips's $E = MO^2$ and Steven Wright's *I Have a Pony*. I could also sing every Python song, and recite, word-perfect, the "Bookshop" sketch off of Monty Python's *Contractual Obligation Album*. Come senior year, I did "Bookshop" in a forensics competition. Both voices, back and forth. That was the first time I experienced, if only secondhand, the effect that *doing* comedy had on the comedian. The laugh you get after dropping your joke is akin to a rush of emotional heroin after the nerve-scraping silence of the setup. That's how the addiction begins. But unlike a common junkie, you crave the discomfort as much as you do the high. The risk of that silence sputtering into nothing, or, worse, anger and jeering from an audience, is what makes the

---

*Four seconds.

laughter that much sweeter. And you keep chasing that scenario where you artificially set up the . . .

. . . deadly, deafening, jarring SILENCE . . .

—and then the—

. . . *gentle, roaring-through-your-veins surf-crash of* LAUGHTER.

And "chasing that scenario" meant going onstage, over and over again. Except in my case—my frightened, self-doubting, raised-in-the-suburban-Nerf, penned-veal timidity that I've fought my whole life—going onstage first meant going *to* stages. And watching. Like I'm doing now, in the New Beverly. I have no idea, sitting here in the dark in May of 1995, that the watching will stretch into four years.

And why would I? It didn't take me four years of watching, as a wannabe stand-up, before I hopped onstage. I mean, there were nineteen years of absorption, but did that count? Then there was a Christmas visit to San Francisco when I was eighteen years old, with my family. We stayed at the Marines Memorial Club and Hotel, and around the corner at Mason and Geary, in a space now inhabited by a jazz club, was an Improv.

I walked down, talked the doorman (Dave Becky, who would briefly be a future manager of mine) into letting me slide by the twenty-one-and-older restriction and watched a show. Pro showcase. Short sets. Solid, forgettable material in front of happy tourists. But even in the blandness of a weeknight showcase of airline food and cats vs. dogs and men vs. women boilerplate stand-up, there was still the simple, addicting solute underneath it. SILENCE/

laughter. I'd tasted the drug in high school. Now I was visiting the equivalent of a junkie's shooting gallery. The pallor of the comedians' skin, their free-for-performers nacho-and-rail-drinks breath, their constant brushes with instant failure and annihilation—none of it drove me away. I wanted in.

I'm feeling the same pull, here in the New Beverly, watching William Holden floating facedown in the pool at the beginning of *Sunset*, the police flashlights knifing around him while his voice-over fills the icy theater air.

How ballsy! That's the *beginning* of the movie! Seriously, what an all-chips-on-one-spin way to start a film! I want to do that. It won't take long, I say to myself, hearing the buttered thunder crunch of another mouthful of popcorn in my ears. Maybe a year, tops, of My Training here at the New Beverly, and I'll be aiming a lens at something that will *swoop.*

A year after my visit to the San Francisco Improv I was a nineteen-year-old college sophomore. I spent my summer weeknights watching open-mikers at Garvin's in Washington, DC. Professionals would drop by every now and then but Tuesdays and Wednesdays at Garvin's were a raw meat duty-dance. My first Tuesday watching a show some skinny guy named Blaine Capatch made a Harlan Ellison reference during his set. No one I'd grown up with read Ellison, let alone knew who he was. Now here was this guy, using him as a casual reference. In the same show Mark Voyce—later to be my roommate—said, mock-jovially, "You know, it takes all kinds." Then his voice shifted to a Balmer-accent diesel bark: "No, it don't.

13

We just *have* all kinds." I was an H. L. Mencken junkie all through high school, but I'd *never* heard his worldview distilled into such a single, elegant dart. And there was fourteen-year-old Dave Chappelle, who performed onstage like he'd been doing comedy for forty years.

I watched them stalk the stage and bomb, or stand still and slay, or a combination of both. They seemed as delighted by the failures as they did by the successes. But these weren't successes or failures with the same pace or flavor as those you'd experience during a week in an office cubicle. I was certain of *that*, at least—I was spending eight hours of zombie time in a legal firm Monday through Friday. No, those successes and failures had a secondhand flavor and a mine cart's pace. They only affected you insofar as they made someone *else* succeed or fail. And they were stretched out and diluted—first over the space of a week, then months and years and, before you realized it, over the span of a life you were looking back on with rage and exhaustion.

But once you walked onstage you rented, if only for five minutes, a kingdom where you owned the air, you owned time, you owned silence, you owned attention and indifference and defeat and failure. If you could master that kingdom, you could trade up for bigger and bigger kingdoms. It wasn't a fair marketplace you traded in, and there were plenty of people who built their kingdoms solidly, only to see them usurped and diminished by bold thieves, fleeting flavors and the chummily mediocre, but it wasn't any more harsh than the cubicle world. At least, that's how I saw it. Like I was seeing it now, in the New

Beverly, when Norma Desmond suddenly stands up and thrusts a rebuking hand into the glowing chrome beam of a movie projector, demanding that time and silence come under her thrall again. Even if you know *nothing* about the process of filmmaking (as I do at that moment), you can sense the fear, excitement and risk that went into a scene like that—for the writer to conceive it, for the director to facilitate it, for the actors to execute it and for the editor to hinge it to the flow of a thousand other moments with as much gambled on them.

And even more than the thrill of the stage, there was the Hang.

Before and after sets, waiting to go on or coming down off the high (or swimming up through the low) of a set, comedians talked to each other in a coded cant that I craved over the warmed-over catchphrase chatter of the cubicle. I copped, immediately, to one of the first and most enduring bonuses to being a comedian: *you got to hang out with comedians.* You sat by the source of the jokes. You saw them get formed and could maybe add to or refine them. The back-and-forth, the jousting and competition, and the heat it emitted. Another vent of creativity, hidden in the darkness. Instead of one silvery movie screen, you were in a forest of agile, hyper-wired minds. I imagine newsrooms, cop bars and marine platoons have the same hum. And if you pick up that frequency, you're saved. And doomed.

I wanted to be doomed.

I will not trust a comedian who doesn't hang out with other comedians. Or who doesn't really have any comedian friends. Or worse, if they *do* have comedian friends,

15

they make sure their friends are less funny, and less successful, than they are. Because they must suspect (or learned early) that nothing funny, startling or original is ever going to fly out of their minds. Why be reminded by the stony, unimpressed faces of the most talented of your tribe? Better to rely on the love of fans and sycophants who, you hope, don't know better.

Watching those first few open mikes before I stoked my courage, I couldn't figure out what I was more excited by: the Stage or the Hang.

So on July 18, 1988, I made the leap. A god-awful five-minute set at Garvin's, in front of—and I'm being generous—twelve people. Jokes about Mike Tyson, jokes about Gummi Bears and jokes about being nervous. Yuck.

And then one joke—it was barely a joke, come to think of it. It was only an idea. Something you'd let float in the air during a Hang, see if anyone responded, bat it around, riff anything off of it.

"I think they should replace the word *of* with the word *o*. It'd make life a lot less serious. Like, if a wife comes home, and she's upset, and her husband's like, 'What's wrong, sweetie?'"

Here came the drop: "And she says, 'The doctor says I have cancer o' the cervix.' *Huh!* That doesn't sound so bad!"

A single laugh. And it was from a comedian. Mark Voyce. And when I say a single laugh, I mean it was a barking, mirthless "Hah!" Which, I was to discover, was how comedians laughed at each other's jokes. We're so inside our heads, thinking of the set we're about to do, or the one we just did, that the objectively stated *hah*, like a nod between

16

samurai, is some of the highest praise you can hope for. It's a way of saying, "Despite how deeply I'm living in my own head right now, and thinking about my jokes, you've just said something that punched through that Wall of Me."

And it was all I needed to doom me forever. Since that night—leading all the way up to this afternoon in May, sitting in the New Beverly—a week hasn't gone by where I haven't gotten up on a stage at least four times a week. Usually closer to ten. Seven years, and never a week without shows, somewhere.

That streak is about to end. I sit here, as *Ace in the Hole* winds down to its final, twilight-before-oblivion shot of Kirk Douglas slumped at his desk, with no future and not a garlic pickle in sight. I have the same feeling I had back in San Francisco at the Improv, and then a year later at Garvin's in DC. I glimpse—in black and white, and not the garish primary-colored sport coats and T-shirts of late-eighties American stand-up—another world I want to enter. What is their Hang like, the directors? What is their thieves' cant? Did Wilder's fellow directors recognize the genius of *Ace in the Hole* in its day? Did they know it instinctually, or was it years of labor before they could see through paltry box office and negative reviews to something that would last beyond the momentary inferno of failure? The same way comedians would watch Andy Kaufman, and then Larry David and Colin Quinn, marveling at the grace and balls it took to completely disregard the audience, to always go for broke with every line? It's one thing to do it onstage—it's you alone, soaring or sinking. But a *movie*? Weeks and months and years of collective labor by talented people in front of and behind the camera? How do you convince anyone to take that sort of risk and then maintain that commitment through all of the bad days of shooting, all of the hopeless hours in the editing room? How do you convince anyone to ever work with you again? What kind of person does that cauldron pressure produce, over time?

I step out into the infant twilight of a Saturday evening in Los Angeles and begin my first full week of not going onstage in seven years. There are stages I can hit tonight, too. If not to perform, to watch. Someone great, someone shitty, it doesn't matter. The great ones show you what you can get away with. The shitty ones remind you what never to bother with.

Instead I go back to my apartment at Normandie and Hollywood, just up the block from the LITTLE ARMENIA and THAI TOWN signs, forever in cross-angled conflict. I get out my copies of *The Film Noir Encyclopedia* and all three volumes of Danny Peary's *Cult Movies* as well as the Necronomicon of Z-grade celluloid—Michael Weldon's indispensable *Psychotronic Encyclopedia of Film.* I want to read up, in classic fledgling-movie-junkie style, on the movies I've just seen. There's *Sunset Boulevard* in *Cult Movies* volume 1, with Peary's usual loving, combative praise. There's *Ace in the Hole*, under the title *The Big Carnival*,* in *The Film Noir Encyclopedia.*

*Films rereleased under different titles. Another annoying, alienating weapon in my film fiend conversational spray. "Yeah, I saw a cheap print of Franju's *Eyes Without a Face*, under the title *The Horror Chamber of Doctor Faustus.* Must've been a print that got sent out

As I read about them an idea strikes me. I get out a pencil and, after etching in a dark, graphite-gray star next to each title, I note the date and location of where I saw it. A star, "5/20/95" and "New Beverly Cinema" go next to *Sunset Boulevard*'s entry in *Cult Movies*. The same for *Ace in*—well, *The Big Carnival*—in *The Film Noir Encyclopedia*.

And for no reason save for the fact that these are the five volumes in front of me as I sit cross-legged on my living room floor, I decided that part of My Training will be to see how many titles I can star, date and place-name in these books. *These five books.* At the time, I'm thinking, "*How many in* one year?"

And on Tuesday, instead of going up and doing a set like I usually do, trying to hone my skills as a comedian, I find myself back at the New Beverly. You see, *The Nutty Professor* is playing. And it's listed in both *The Psychotronic Encyclopedia* and volume 1 of *Cult Movies*. So, I mean, I *have* to see it. To, you know . . . check it off.

I won't even learn that much from watching *The Nutty Professor*, an exhausting comedy made by an exhausted man. Jerry Lewis, in the getting-to-know-you phase of his Percocet addiction, wrestles with the two-headed snake of his loathing of Dean Martin's soul and his thirst to live Dino's life. It's an ice-water-on-bare-skin naked shock, watching Jerry's id play out in that movie. I sit in the New

---

on the drive-in movie circuit in the sixties. Imagine some poor yokel, killing an evening with a double bill, when *Les Yeux Sans Visage* gets slung at him after half-snoozing through *The Alligator People*! Hey, where're you goin'?"

Beverly, letting Jerry Lewis's nasal cri de coeur bounce off of me, thinking of all the loud, aggressive, alpha-clown comedians I'd been stuck with on the road. It is nothing I ever want to do on-screen.

I'm in Los Angeles, with a steady writing job on weekdays at *MADtv*, a dozen "alternative comedy" spaces to go up in and work on material—and now this, the New Beverly, my $5-a-night film school.

Pretty good trio of films to start off my education with, right? *Sunset Boulevard*—a cynical, heartbroken writer, dragged to his doom by a true believer in the illusion of film. *Ace in the Hole*—a satanic, exploitative reporter who picks apart a dying man at the bottom of a pit in the hope that his career will rise back into the sun. And *The Nutty Professor*—an ignored nerd who's tempted by popular monstrosity. Obsession, darkness and magical thinking. Sitting in my apartment late in the night, penciling the star, date and venue name next to *The Nutty Professor* in two film books, I will have no idea I've entered my fourth Night Café.

It will be four years before I pull myself out of it.

CHAPTER TWO

My First Four
Night Cafés

Arles, France,
September 1888

Credit: Michael Meehan

Here's where I explain what I meant when I said "Night Café" back at the end of the last chapter. We have to go way back for the explanation, but it won't take long. Just to the end of summer 1888.

I love the end of summer, by the way. The hellish wick

of August, beginning to yield to the waiting fall. Leaves finally surrendering their green, the sky having one last furnace exhalation before it's safe for a coat to show its face in the afternoon. So this is a pungent, rancid shank of history we're about to gnaw on, the awfulness of August 1888.

Seriously, *what* was in the air in the dying summer of 1888? Did our planet pass through some gigantic, ghostly comet? One that hissed and emitted pure evil? What hung off of the twilight mist and, in the morning, rustled out of view at the first hint of sunlight?

On September 4 of 1888 George Eastman registered the trademark, and also clinched the patent, for his roll camera film. Five days earlier, on August 31, Jack the Ripper left the throat-slit, butcher-gutted body of Mary Ann Nichols on the bricks of Buck's Row in London's East End. Fast-forward to September 8—four days *after* Kodak film existed in the world. The body of Annie Chapman was dumped in a Whitechapel doorway.

Three more victims followed. As did the world's first motion picture. *Roundhay Garden Scene*—a two-second film by Louis Le Prince. Four people in a garden. Two men, two women. There, on the left, a man in a dark suit takes gentlemanly strides past a woman in a smart white dress. She shifts her feet, turns and takes a step away from the camera. And there on the right, the other couple. A stout woman in a dark dress who appears to walk backward. And circling around her, at a less gentlemanly, more predatory pace, a man in a white, duster-length overcoat and hat. We never see his face. A circling wraith, captured on celluloid.

No photographs of Jack the Ripper. No movies, either—not even a two-second blip, maybe of his dropping the bloody fragment of Catherine Eddowes's apron after he killed her on September 30. Whatever was infecting the crisp air near the end of 1888 evaded being captured on film.

It didn't escape oil and canvas, though.

In that same September, in the city of Arles—in the south of France and snuggled by the Mediterranean Sea—Vincent van Gogh painted a masterpiece that destroyed him.

Vincent van Gogh was a "tormented genius" the way Jimi Hendrix was a "guitar player." I remember, reading Stephen King's *On Writing*, when he said something about how "your art needs to be a function of your life, not the other way around." Van Gogh's art had moved beyond being a "function" of his life and had metastasized into a tumor that was keeping him alive only to kill him more slowly. But in Arles, Vincent decided to take control of his "art." Except that he made it hurry up with the task of his annihilation.

It didn't help that Vincent was a religious fanatic. And, again, not to hit the "tormented genius" comparison again, but his career as a simple country priest was cut short when his parishioners were appalled at his intensity, his Saint Francis of Assisi–like commitment to squalor, poverty and filth. His flock wanted Huey Lewis and the News—what they got was GG Allin and the Murder Junkies. And his religious fervor spread to his art, the way cancer will spread to other organs of a sufferer's body. He had a gift—the gift of transcendent artistic talent. But his religious convictions made him feel that this talent was demonic, and something to be ashamed and frightened of.

What to do? Simple—he only ever painted *what he saw*. What he was specifically looking at while he painted. He was only creating a representation of the world as it presented itself before his eyes. See? Demonic forces kept at bay, artistic itch scratched. Win-win.

For a while. Any true creative endeavor demands constant evolution, growth, experimentation and challenge. As the summer of 1888 bloomed and ripened and then rotted in the August heat, Vincent van Gogh walked the earth feeling like a rusty cage barely holding a cackling, paint-stained legion of bright, gibbering demons.

And so, to Arles. A change of scenery—*that* was the solution! A whole city full of people and places and objects he'd never seen before! More cordwood for the demons to burn away to ash.

And it didn't help. "They change their sky, not their soul, who run across the sea." That was Horace in 65 BC. A truism that applies so perfectly to every one of my friends who leave L.A. for New York, and find themselves a year later with newly toned legs from walking, scraped-raw nerves from the assault that is Manhattan, and a sudden yearning to ". . . I dunno, move upstate, or maybe to Williamsburg."

Van Gogh didn't even have a Williamsburg. Arles was going to need to save him *and* propel him forward. That combination rarely happens in quotidian existence. In art? It's as rare as Sasquatch riding a unicorn.

But, after first arriving, it seemed that Vincent might have pulled it off. The town offered endless, gorgeous sights for him to capture in thick, manic gobs of oil on canvas. Starry, starry night skies, lush interiors, peaceful street scenes where the sea-scrubbed air gave the atmosphere the tickly tingle of a daydream.

And something even better happened for him, in terms of artistic inspiration. His friend, ex-accountant turned Tahitian layabout artist Paul Gauguin, suggested something radical. Why not paint something . . . *from memory*? Just once, instead of painting what you're *actually* looking at, render an artwork through the prism of recollection. What newer, emotional details might surface through the rigid, unyielding mesh of religion and shame that you've used to bind that throbbing, genius brain of yours? Vincent, give it a try.

And he did. *The Night Café*, painted in September of 1888. While George Eastman made it possible to forever trap reality on paper, while Jack the Ripper carved, in flesh wounds, a ragged peephole into the twentieth century, van Gogh painted from memory. And it destroyed him.

The first time I saw *The Night Café* was in college, during a psychology class. We were watching a slide show about the artwork of schizophrenics. About how certain characteristics appeared, over and over again, in their work. Distorted perspective. Faceless figures. Light sources with what appeared to be cartoon "stink lines" emanating from them, as if the painter could see (or feel? or hear? or smell and taste?) the beams of illumination cutting through the darkness.

And in the middle of the slide show of crude, crayon-on-construction-paper renderings, saved from the trash bins of countless mental hospitals, there clicked into view van Gogh's *The Night Café*.

It kicked me in the head. Even looking at it from the middle of a lecture hall, a distant, projected transparency on a classroom screen, the menace and magic of that painting grabbed me. Tendrils of glistening paint whipped out, snagged my eyeballs, and held fast.

Go look at *The Night Café*, if you have any access—art book, Internet, anything. This was van Gogh's memory of the Café de la Gare in Arles. Probably a seedy place, but not unpleasant. A room where drunks and derelicts could rent a chair against the cold of night for the price of a glass of brandy. Could, perhaps, sleep off a day's self-abuse on the crook of an arm on a tabletop. Gauguin painted it, later, in much sunnier tones.

But that's not how van Gogh remembered it. Or saw it. Or saw all of life, it seems. Whatever piloted his body from inside the blue-eyed skull of van Gogh rarely saw a pretty planet.

Look at *The Night Café*. See the red walls, like the color of butchered meat, or the inside of a carcass during an autopsy? See the lines coming off of the yellow lamps on the ceiling, almost as if they're screaming? The way the pool table seems to crouch, like some badly constructed hell-beast, about to lurch out of the drawing at you? The faceless waiter, in his spotless whites, struggling to stand upright and human while surrounded with the hunched-over gargoyle figures of the café's denizens? And finally the overall, claustrophobic architecture of the room, of the building, like evil itself is outside, softening the building's timbers with hot saliva and warping the framework inward through need and rage. George Eastman's camera filmed garden parties and bridges. Van Gogh's paintbrush captured, like a Q-tip swabbing a germ-filled throat culture, a sample of the dirty darkness loose in the air at the end of 1888. There it is, on the canvas of *The Night Café*. Murder-vibe tentacles, coiling out around your eyes and muddying your heart.

Van Gogh entered a room in his mind when he painted *The Night Café*. He acknowledged his damaged (and worsening) psyche and, in acknowledging it, made a deal. He would be able to take newer, more original artistic conceptions out, would be able to capture them in paintings. His psyche found the deal acceptable. It let Vincent leave the room—the Night Café—with vistas and visions he hadn't come close to before in his career. But something followed him out, and latched on to him like a virus, and he was never the same.

He was a better painter. A transformed one. Masterpieces flew out of him like pigeons from a condemned cathedral. *Starry Night over the Rhône, The Yellow House, Bedroom in Arles, Les Arènes*—all before Christmas of 1888.

Of course, by Christmas Eve Vincent was battering his head against the walls of the Old Hospital in Arles, having severed his ear and given it to a prostitute named Rachel. By February of 1889, after he'd been released from the Old Hospital a *second* time, the townspeople of Arles circulated a petition, demanding that Vincent be confined permanently. Van Gogh fled to Saint-Rémy-de-Provence (and the Saint-Paul asylum) shortly thereafter. One year later, in the summer of 1890, Vincent ended his life with a gunshot wound to the chest. It took him a day and a half to die. That sort of profound insanity pays dividends—in hideous endurance and terrible tenacity.

·····

"I told you that story to tell you this one."

That's Bill Cosby, again, off of his *Revenge* album. I know it seems like I'm taking a roundabout way to explain what I mean by *Night Café*, but everything I just laid out was to get you ready for the fact that I've had *six* of them.

None of them drove me mad. I still have both ears. My chest cavity is bullet-free.

But the concept of the Night Café—the room you enter, and then leave having been forever changed—is an abiding, repeated event in my life. Six times, so far, it's happened to me. All of them had to do with my creativity, and my imagination, and how I saw the world and my place in it. Here are the first four:

The Tustin Library in Tustin, California, 1974

I've written about this, at length, in my last book, *Zombie Spaceship Wasteland*. So here's a quick summation.

Nineteen seventy-four. Halloween. Five years old. Kids'

day at the library. Ghost stories and pumpkin cookies and witches made out of construction paper. And a movie!

With zero malice on their part, the adults who organized the afternoon showed F. W. Murnau's 1922 film *Nosferatu*. They closed the blinds on the windows and projected it against a bare wall. Eight-millimeter film, clattering projector, that faint burning smell as the projector bulb ignited the microscopic dust particles. Dust particles are mostly flakes of dead human skin. So, when I was five, I watched *Nosferatu* with the atavistic, pagan odor of simmering flesh corkscrewing itself into my memory. The optics are dream-logic, ratman vampire imagery. The perfume is cannibal cookout. That little square of light took over that darkened room, and while I and the other kids around me screamed and cried,* I wanted onto the other side of that screen. By hook or by crook (as it turned out, by stage and by book), I'd do it.

At five years old, I left my first Night Café. With nightmares and a pumpkin cookie.

Garvin's Comedy Club, 1988

Yes, that room full of overpriced potato skins, puerile dick jokes and watered-down drinks was my second Night Café. I went in thinking stand-up comedy would be one of a dozen things I'd try before I settled on what I would

---

*Show your kids *Irreversible*, *Salo* or *The Last Temptation of Christ* before you show them *any* silent film. Even the benign ones are unintended windows into stuttery, subconscious terror rhythms.

do with my life. During that summer I also worked as a sportswriter (under my own name) and a columnist (under a fake name—"Hartman Dreadstone") for a small, local paper. I worked as a paralegal trainee during the day. And a party deejay on weekends. Any one of those paid better and gave me more positive reinforcement than the four minutes of silence and one single laugh at Garvin's that night. But I left changed. Another Night Café. I wanted to be a comedian. I wanted to hang out with comedians. I wanted to be lunar, not solar. A tiny step toward the other side of that screen I'd seen when I was five.

The Holy City Zoo, May 1992

Another comedy club. Like Garvin's. Except not at all like Garvin's. The polar opposite. Between Garvin's in Washington, DC, and the Holy City Zoo in San Francisco, California—somewhere on the highway I drove west across the United States on in 1992—there was a magical portal. Tornado or tollbooth, wardrobe or rabbit hole. I have no idea. But I'm glad I tumbled through it.

By the summer of 1992 I'd been doing comedy four years and was jock-confident about my skills and progress. That first night at Garvin's? One laugh? Well, those days were long behind me. I was starting to feature—and in some cases, headline—at some of the finest comedy clubs on the East Coast and in the eastern Midwest. Sir Laffs-a-Lot; the Shaft in Norton, Virginia; and Slapstix (the "x" meant "brace yourself for 'x'-citement!"). I had surefire bits about tampon commercials, movie theater popcorn, farts, superheroes farting and shooting things out of their ass, and masturbating. And farting. Four years into my career and I was pulling in a hefty $7,000 a year—and these were 1992 dollars! Yeah, I'd moved back in with my parents after a year in Baltimore, but that's only because I wanted to save money for my big move to the West Coast. Once I made it to the shores of the Pacific, my surefire brand of chuckle-making would rocket me straight onto an HBO special. A sitcom would follow. How could it not? *Patton Pending? Generally Patton? Oswalt My Gum?*

That's the attitude I had on Wednesday, May 6, 1992, when I first entered the Holy City Zoo in San Francisco. I'd moved there the day before. My wheezing Volkswagen Jetta had dropped its water pump onto a mountain road outside Truckee, California. All of the money I'd saved by moving back in with my parents went toward getting it fixed. I was moths-in-pockets broke, sharing an apartment with two other comedians. My room was the living room. My bed was a futon on the floor. One of my roommates, Carlos Alazraqui, was destined to be the voice of the Taco Bell Chihuahua. I was destined to go onstage at the legendary Holy City Zoo, my second night in San Francisco, and announce myself as the new gunslinger in town. Hadn't I done my time in the countryside, training like a duelist, quickening my draw and honing my aim until all enemies fell when I slapped leather and fanned the hammer?

Oh, the cheap, cinematic victory I replayed over and over in my head as I walked down Clement Street that night, notebook under my arm.

I was dressed for battle, too. I learned, from my four years walking the giggle-shack latitudes, how to dress. Sport coat, ripped jeans and sneakers. Years ago, in Philadelphia, a comedy club owner told me, when I dared to go onstage wearing a Flaming Carrot Comics T-shirt, not to "ever wear anything that can distract from your jokes." Sage advice from a man who always slayed with the exact same twelve minutes the entire four years I knew him. I streamlined my act along the same lines, as well as my wardrobe. Now, tonight, for my crushing debut, I had a blue polka-dot shirt from Eddie Bauer; a bolo tie with a muted, abstract, brick-red scorpion as a clasp; and silver aglets. My jeans only had a few tears in them, and I wore black Chuck Taylors. I mean, how could anyone who even *glanced* at me not recognize this avatar of awesomeness they shared the planet with?

When you walked into the Holy City Zoo, you passed through two swinging doors into a room that had "vertical" and "narrow" to spare. "Wide" and "spacious"—not so much. A tiny bar to your left, a postage-stamp stage immediately beyond it. Seating for an audience of fifty, if it was packed. And, as if put there as a prank, an opera-style pair of elevated box seats to stage left. They held two people. Anyone who sat there drew more focus than anyone who was onstage.

The Holy City Zoo did comedy every single night of the week. Not just the Tuesday-maybe-Wednesday open mikes, with booked, professional Friday and Saturday shows like the clubs I worked, first in DC and then up and down the East Coast. *Every single night*, there was something at the Zoo. Open mikes Mondays and Tuesdays and, like tonight, sometimes Wednesdays. Other times Wednesdays were taken up by sketch or improv groups or . . . something. Friday and Saturday, sometimes Sunday—the pros, making money, drawing crowds of fifty. I was sure I'd be headlining those nights before 1992 was over.

Hey—it was looking pretty crowded. Lot of people there. They looked like civilians, too. Not comedians. Jeans, T-shirts. Maybe a button-up shirt over the T-shirt. They were probably waiting to get drinks before they sat down. I couldn't wait to rock their worlds. Hadn't I done that already, to sold-out crowds at Charlie Goodnight's in Raleigh, North Carolina? I mean, the show was sold out because I was opening for Bill Hicks, sure, but I proved I belonged up there, killing it with my no-fail closing bit about the Cookie Monster if he were gay. Hadn't Bill been gracious and polite to me, even speaking to me once between shows? He recognized a future great when he saw one, sure. No way was he trying to fill the awkward silence as I stared at him over my free-for-comedians soda, wondering how he slaughtered using a third of the energy I was so desperately putting out.

None of the crowd at the Holy City Zoo was taking their seats. Oh, wait. Well, *those* three people did. A young couple and a strange-looking older man with a bag of peanut M&M's that he ate, robotically, while staring off into space. Hopefully, more people would sit down before the show started. I found the sign-up sheet so I could add my name— Oh, hold on. There were already seventeen names before mine. Where were all the comedians? Were you supposed to come in early? Did they sign up hours ago and then go to get dinner or something? Why didn't anyone tell me?

I added my name to the list and found a place at the bar where I could lean and check my notes and watch the show. The bar was crowded and most of the audience still hadn't taken a seat.

It took me a moment to realize that almost all of them were taking out notebooks, jotting down jokes, getting ready.

These were the comedians.

They were dressed just like they'd dress in real life. Flannel shirts, blank T-shirts, work boots. Like they'd walked, midconversation, from the sidewalk to the stage.

Blaine Capatch sat down at the bar beside me. We'd driven out a few weeks apart. The year before, Blaine had traveled out to San Francisco and returned to the East Coast with tales of wonder. Stages everywhere! Comedians our age, getting work! Cheap rent! Cheaper food! Strong coffee! Bookstores and sushi and fog and weed—right there for the taking, instead of in odd, out-of-the-way Baltimore neighborhoods or a single block in DC. The few pockets of strangeness that we took humming-bird-like sips from back home were simply part of the everyday scenery in San Francisco. I dreamed of standing at the corner where Miles Archer takes three slugs in the belly at the beginning of *The Maltese Falcon*, sipping an espresso machiatto and thinking deep thoughts in the chill mist.

"Isn't this place great?" said Blaine. He was dressed in his usual all black, looking the way every New Wave keyboard player wished they looked. Blaine had a Zen mind inside of a switchblade body. He fit right in. I already resented him.

"Yeah. I feel like the ghost of Lenny Bruce is going to walk through the doors."

Blaine said, "You're thinking of the Hungry I."

I winced. "You're right."

The show started. Every comedian was young. A few were "older" than me, in that they were twenty-three or twenty-four.

They did jokes in a way I'd never seen comedians do jokes in my four years of comedy. At Garvin's, on an open-mike night and even when I went pro and started working weekends, the only thing that mattered was the end result. If someone got laughs, and got rebooked, and made money? That was the end of the aesthetic argument. There was no such thing as "hack" comedy back where I started. There was only "working" and "not working." I remember very clearly, one night in 1990 during a comedy competition in Newport News, I pointed to a comedian on the cover of a magazine. I opined that maybe she wasn't the funniest person currently doing comedy. Every other comedian in the room turned on me. I was suddenly a rare steak in a hyena cage. "I don't see *you* on the cover of a magazine. She's on the *cover of a magazine*. So she's funny." There was no comeback for me—at least, not in my addled, mulleted, twenty-one-year-old head.

Now I was sitting in a dark, narrow chamber, an odd

room that felt like a tiny, hidden lobe of the world's brain. Incarnate on the tiny stage, of that tiny room, was every retort and answer to that Newport News assault. Every answer to why it doesn't fucking matter if you get rich or famous *without* the funny was up on the stage that night, *enjoying* being comedians. No HBO specials on the horizon, no sitcom dreams, not even mainstream club headlining gigs. They wanted to do comedy for the sake of doing comedy. I hadn't seen that yet, in my career. I'd seen little glimpses of it, within my tiny circle of friends back on the East Coast. Blaine, and Mark, and Dave, and our friend Jeff Hatz. And me. But we were treated like mutants. We *thought* we were mutants, and for whatever few moments of genuine risk and weirdness we allowed ourselves, we also had our sights on fitting in and thriving in middle-of-the-road, mozzarella-sticks-and-comment-cards comedy clubs. We could at least argue that we belonged in the Hang since we were earning the Money, getting the Bookings.

Now I saw the perfect antithesis of that, comedian after comedian, at the Holy City Zoo. Jim Earl and Barry Lank, a comedy duo with Bob & Ray's genialness, channeling Carl Panzram's murderous misanthropy. Greg Behrendt, doing an extended riff about Jimi Hendrix's secret sideline as a pastry chef that made absolutely no sense and absolutely cracked my shit up. Laura Milligan—who was Nancy Spungen with Gore Vidal's brain. Greg Proops, a snide superego who could make you piss yourself simply with the way he said the name "Adolphe *Menjou*," like a dirty in-joke both of you were sharing in a foxhole. Warren Thomas (RIP), as shocked and delighted by his own seat-of-the-pants improvisations as the audience was. Kurt Weitzmann—casually, breezily blasphemous. Maybe you know some of these names. Maybe you don't. They were all—and still are, to me—crucial.

The comedians would finish their sets and sit or lean against the wall or huddle at the bar and watch the rest of the show. There was an energy in that room I never got to experience at *any* East Coast open mike—a feeling of delight in the silence as much as the laughter. If I'd become a junkie after my first open mike at Garvin's, four years ago, then I was now hanging out with steel-skinned freebasers.*

Blaine went up. Pretty good. But something was wrong. His more esoteric references and odd non sequiturs got *way* bigger laughs than his killer "A" material. I was confused for a moment, and then allowed myself a shimmer of smugness that came more from the fear that he'd eclipse me and leave me behind in this new city. I told myself, *He's just not delivering his jokes with any real conviction. He's not* selling *them. I'm a headliner. A* head-

---

*I should probably point out here that when I say "East Coast" I mean Virginia, and North Carolina and Maryland and Delaware. I never made it up to New York between 1988 and 1992. Not to Boston, either. And Chicago? Unthinkable. Never had the money, couldn't get the bookings. And I was also kind of a pussy. Like I said earlier, I was a suburban-raised veal. Imperviousness to the honk and hustle of big cities was a callus I hadn't grown yet. Too bad—the same thing I'm describing here, in San Francisco in 1992, was happening on an even more intense, profound level in New York, Boston and Chicago. I would have been chewed up even worse in those cities. I hope that's not too much of a spoiler. Keep reading—I'm sure you can tell, but this gets ugly.

lining comedian. *I know how to sell a solid set, no matter what the audience.*

Blaine ended to solid applause from the other comedians. They knew him, remembered him from the previous summer. No one doesn't like Blaine Capatch.

Three more comedians went up and then it was my spot. I only had to do five to seven minutes. I mean, I've got an hour of solid-gold, can't-miss material, right? For a moment I flashed to Jack Nicholson as the Joker in Tim Burton's *Batman*, lit from below and sneering over a blood-streaked newspaper about the Dark Knight's terrorizing Gotham's criminal.

"Terrorizes? Wait'll they get a load of me."

Yep, those were the strip-mall psych-up strategies I'd run in my head back then, but they'd worked so far, hadn't they? This audience was *mine*.

And up I went. I forget who the emcee was.

But they are very pleasant as they read my name and ask the audience to welcome me and I step to the mike stand and I pivot not speaking immediately I'd learned that you see you don't just rush to the mike and start telling jokes like you're terrified you'll lose them right off the bat you take a moment show them you belong up there you're *confident* and they're in good hands they can relax and let themselves be taken *anywhere you want to take them* and then I clear my throat and look down at the stool next to me and it hits me all of a sudden I'm the *only* comedian besides Blaine who didn't go up onstage with a notebook I wanted to show them I had my act all memorized I was a professional and ready with the jokes *locked and loaded* so here comes one look right out of the chute hi I'm Patton Oswalt and I'm cute and cuddly which I say with the same inflection I perfected out on the road and usually just saying that itself gets a laugh and puts me at ease 'cause I know I've got a killer line to say afterward but what in the fuck there's nothing *nothing* not even a chuckle and so I say too quick I don't pause enough like I do when the audience is responding I say you know what THAT means right and before I can let them answer I too quick let tumble out can't get laid 'cause when a girl says you're cute and cuddly it's like she's saying oh you're like Teddy Ruxpin let me stick a tape cassette up your ass and you can talk to me while I fall asleep and it's hitting me now after seeing everyone else go up that *holy fuck* that isn't even really a joke at all it's a set of words designed to get a laugh from people who aren't really listening who are half-drunk and wondering when the fried shrimp are going to get there I just heard the comedian say *laid* and *Teddy Ruxpin* and *ass* and I guess that means there's a joke there so ha ha ha only this isn't the kind of crowd I'm performing for now in the Holy City Zoo it's other comedians funny comedians who give a shit how they write their jokes and none of them went for easy laughs and this is the way I'm announcing myself in a new city *no* risk *no* thought nothing to see here and I get dry-mouthed and rush right into the next joke something about Bob Dylan performing at Kings Dominion but that's an amusement park in Virginia no one here knows what the fuck Kings Dominion is but I'm just hurrying to the Bob Dylan impression which is also a surefire laugh and when things are starting out shitty a way for me to buy myself a little breathing room but again nothing not a peep why the fuck would they care about a Bob Dylan *impression* especially after seeing Greg Behrendt's more conceptual smarter Jimi Hendrix stuff so I go into a story about having a hernia operation last year which totally didn't happen it's a fucking lie but there's all these funny jokes about bedpans and the drugs they give you and still nothing so now I'm three and a half minutes into what's supposed to be a seven-minute set and I go into my killer closer about the tampon commercials with that never-fail punch line Tampax we're not number one but we're up there and this gets a fucking *groan* of course why would it not it's so fucking shitty and I say good night and walk off the stage like I've had my shins shot off.

Hello, San Francisco! There's a new kid in town!

Blaine and I watched the rest of the show. When the show ended we mingled. Blaine seemed to know everyone. Greg Behrendt tried to be friendly but he couldn't help looking at my bolo tie and saying, "Really?"

Everyone was leaving. Blaine and I walked across Clement Street to a restaurant called Taiwan. It was the color of an old, pink rose and made the best dim sum I'd ever tasted. It's still there. Go in sometime. Sit at the third table to your right as you pass the hostess station. That's where Blaine and I sat that night, and ordered fried rice, and drank tea, and quietly tore pages out of our notebooks.

Old set lists. Lists of jokes, and concepts and ideas

we were working on. We carefully, methodically, brutally ripped away everything we'd built inside clubs like Garvin's and in a thousand forgotten one-night gigs in bars and restaurants and colleges. By the time our waiter slapped our check on the table, we were the proud owners of blank notebooks. We had no choice. Change or die.

The Holy City Zoo was my third Night Café. I went in wanting to be a comedian. I left wanting to be an artist. I know that's pretentious and grandiose and half of the comedians reading this right now are thinking *Fuck you, poser* but it is the absolute, embarrassing truth. Don't think for a second I don't value my years writing forgettable, passable, meat-and-potatoes jokes on the road. As you'll see, when I reached my fifth Night Café, those four years of hackery saved me.

But for now? In 1992 San Francisco? I needed the dark thought-temple that was the Holy City Zoo to burn my skills to the ground and force me to start over. I experienced complete humiliation in those four and a half minutes—but I also glimpsed a better Hang, whispers of better Stages, and, if I didn't crack or lose faith or just puss out and go home, the possibility of becoming a better comedian. So I spent the next year, over and over again, passing through those swinging doors. I watched. I wrote. I bombed. I bombed less. I wrote more. I started venturing out to the other clubs the city had to offer. Cobb's. The Punch Line. Then outside of the city—Tommy T's and Fubar's and the Punch Line in solid-steel Republican

Walnut Creek.* Slowly, and with way more crash-and-burn.

I unlearned.

So those were Night Cafés one through three. The first one was a projector-bulb beacon, which led to the second one. The second one contained a vocation, which I followed to the third one. The third one—the Holy City Zoo—contained an art. I curse the humiliation and bless the annihilation, and even more valuable than the impulse toward art, I gained an inner radar for dark, hidden places where the strange ones go. That inner beacon led me down to Los Angeles, a little more than three years after my Holy City Zoo debut/flameout. Where I found myself on Beverly Boulevard, in the sunshine, staring at the New Beverly Cinema.

The New Beverly Cinema, May of 1995

I was gonna be a director. The New Beverly Cinema was going to teach me how.

It had better, I thought. I was lucky, but for how long? After three years in San Francisco, I managed to get a staff writing job on *MADtv*. More money than I'd ever seen in my life. More money in two weeks than I'd made in my first *year* as a professional comedian.

*I got to work with Bill Hicks one more time at the Walnut Creek Punch Line. I saw him walk half an audience one night and when one lady barked at him, "Don't you believe in *God*?" he retorted, "I do. I just don't believe in people."

But the boom years of stand-up comedy were over by 1995. I watched the Washington, DC, comedy scene fold up at the end of 1991. The San Francisco scene began collapsing two years later. The Holy City Zoo? Gone. One year after my first set, closed up. A karaoke bar.

"We've been running across a log bridge that's coming apart behind us," said Blaine as we packed up our Lower Haight apartment in April and got ready to drive down to Los Angeles and plant ourselves in an office at Ren-Mar Studios, cranking out sketches like "Gump Fiction" and "Republican Gladiators." We'd still do comedy at night, we told ourselves. More comedians were moving to Los Angeles from San Francisco, and New York and Boston, and they brought a DIY attitude with them. So stages were beginning to appear in coffee shops, and Laundromats, and record stores. We were still a year from someone calling our scene "alternative comedy," so for now, it was simply "comedy not in clubs." I saw a lot of fun and creativity in it. But how the fuck would I keep myself in what Blaine called "rent and ramen"?

So I sat in the New Beverly. And watched. And thought. And retraced. The projector beam when I was five. Garvin's when I was nineteen. The Holy City Zoo when I was twenty-three. The Lure. The Job. The Art. Following the Art had led me to another Job. *MADtv.* An office. A fun job, but it was hard, sometimes, to squeeze Art out of it. I thought comedy club audiences were an impassable firewall. Then I met network executives.

And now the New Beverly Cinema, at twenty-six. Night after night, films by people who'd found a way to make Art and Commerce dance together to whatever tiny tune was playing in their heads. It seemed impossible to me, to make that leap. Too scary. My penned-veal suburban instincts were rearing their heads again. I mean, I had a job. A *really* good job, come to think of it. I couldn't have stayed in San Francisco forever, I told myself. Ultimately, you had to be down in Los Angeles. I'd find peace here. Hadn't Sherman Torgan? Up in his ticket booth, with a million combinations of double features in his head? He lived in San Francisco for a while in the late sixties. Scouted for the studios. Loved movies, like me. But moved back down to Los Angeles. Gotta be where the celluloid is fresh. Opened the New Beverly, kept Art alive. Barely made any money, but he was at peace. Wasn't he?

"You can have peace. Or you can have freedom. Don't ever count on having both at once." Robert Heinlein wrote that. Well, I had neither. I wasn't free at *MADtv*, and I wasn't at peace inside my head.

Because the Holy City Zoo, as much as it made me pursue Art, had also made me jealous and competitive. And not in a good way. Now, at age twenty-six, when I saw a comedian do something brilliant or new? I wasn't energized by it. Not like I had been at Garvin's, when I was nineteen. Now I got threatened and envious and spiteful. Self-sabotaging. Los Angeles in 1995 was becoming a honey lure for writers and comedians who were so much funnier, so much more inventive and quick than I could ever dream of being. I'd fooled myself into thinking I was this young gunslinger, but now I felt like a nerve-blasted old cowboy with a shaky hand and a rusty revolver.

There I was, I thought, at *MADtv*, struggling to explain to a network suit what *Apocalypse Now* was, and how it could be funny if done through the prism of a Rankin Bass special.* Meanwhile, over at HBO's *Mr. Show*, my onetime San Francisco roommate Brian Posehn was writing and performing with Bob Odenkirk (from Chicago) and David Cross (Boston by way of Atlanta). They were changing the form, the way we'd been trying to at the Zoo. How had they willed that impulse onto television? I sure hadn't. I was going to be swept away and forgotten. I'd end up like the sad old local headliners I'd see come into Garvin's on a Tuesday night. Never moved out of their hometown, never stretched their skills. Hopping onstage to massage their egos for seven minutes, and then home to empty calendars, old jokes, compromise.

Remember the bullshit, grandiose victories I could imagine for myself? Well, I could do tragedy even better.

---

*They eventually shot my idea—a year after I left the show. Well, I really didn't leave. They didn't have me back. And with good fucking reason. I was a judgmental, sour asshole of a writer. Quick with a criticism and never with a fix. A comedy and film snob who rolled his eyes half the time and turned in typo-filled scripts. But they shot it. And put my name in the credits. Misspelled. Revenge? They were entitled. The sketch was called "A Pack of Gifts Now," and it was lovingly animated by a stop-motion genius named Corky Quakenbush. An elf is sent by toy makers to the North Pole to terminate "the Kringle" and his cultlike operation of toy makers "with extreme prejudice." And, ironically enough, one of the producers I clashed with, Fax Bahr—who codirected the documentary *Hearts of Darkness*, about the making of . . . *Apocalypse Now*—shepherded the sketch through, with all of my visual jokes and references intact, and plenty of his own, which made the sketch even better. Even got a mention in *TV Guide*. Thanks, Fax. Sorry I was such a dick. Part of being in your twenties is not knowing an ally when you see one.

Brooding in the dark of the New Beverly with Welles and Kurosawa and Bergman all that summer was a day spa for my depression.

I didn't know it, all through the months of self-serving terror and projected panic, but I was soon to enter my fifth Night Café. I couldn't enter it then—mainly because it didn't yet exist.

CHAPTER THREE

The Largo

Los Angeles, 1996

6	7	8	9
MCCoy TYNER TRIO Catalina Grill ✓	GENGHiS COHEN ✓		PeDRO'S GRiLLe ✓
13 Close ENCOUNTERS of the 3rd Kind N. Beverly ✓ UPFRONT COMEDY THeATeR ✓	**14** COLUMBUS DAY (OBSERVED) THANKSGIVING DAY (CANADA) NApoleoN 4 Star ✓	**15** RAiDeRS of the Lost ARK N. Beverly ✓	**16** BOUND Mann's Chinese
20 UNCaBaReT ✓	**21**	**22** Beauty & THe BeasT N. Beverly ✓	**23**
27 DAYLIGHT SAVING TIME ends ← IMPROV →✓ Irvine	**28** THe LaRGO ✓	**29**	**30** "THe DAY the CLOWN CRieD" READiNG ✓

October 22, 1996. I was hunkered down in the New Beverly, while Jean Cocteau's 1946 *Beauty and the Beast* swam across the screen above my head. Living arms holding candelabras reached from walls. Magic pools. Wicks that lit themselves. Time and gravity ignoring the rules of the universe, bending and flexing to the logic of Cocteau's tiny, enclosed eggshell dream theater of a film. Later on I checked off this film in my *Psychotronic Encyclopedia*. Michael Weldon, in his thumbnail description, mentioned how anyone viewing this movie would wonder why people can't make movies today that look *half* as good as this fifty-year-old masterpiece.

Two weeks before this I'd been downtown, at the Orpheum, watching a double bill of *The Man from Planet X* and the original *Night of the Living Dead*. Did George Romero remember those reaching limbs from *Beauty and the Beast* when he made *Dead*—those fish-belly zombie arms insistent through the slats of the farmhouse, where the group of desperate outsiders barricaded themselves against the ravenous waves of flesh eaters? Come to think of it, did Roman Polanski also have that image in his head when he made *Repulsion*, and Catherine Deneuve had her blazing, third-act freak-out?

Connections pinged in my head while I watched. This was how I was consuming movies. More connective tissue the more films I saw. A year plus, since that Saturday spent with Billy Wilder, and almost nightly, I was returning to the New Beverly. And my hunger for films led me to other rep sites, too. Sherman Torgan was cool with that. He was the confident madam of an abiding brothel. There is no sating a film freak's itch for variety. The New Beverly started as a doorway for me, and then became a hub. So I ventured out. First to the then-in-its-infancy American Cinematheque—a pirate operation that roamed from theater to theater, hoping for a home, its final nest in the Egyptian still years away. And then the late, lamented Tales Café (a gorgeous book-closet of a theater with plush, irregular chairs; a 16 mm projector; and stacks and stacks of short story collections—*absolutely no novels*, only short story collections). The mighty Nuart on Santa Monica, one of a chain of Landmark *Thea-tahs** that combined the restored classics with the up-and-comers like Christopher Nolan, Ramin Bahrani and Harmony Korine. And, finally, the impossibly lush, eerily understaffed and inexplicably-supplied-with-the-cleanest-prints-I've-ever-seen Four Star on Wilshire. Chinese Triad? Russian mob? What in God's name was happening there? Where did they find a scratch-and-blemish-free print of Abel Gance's *Napoleon*? Why was the snack bar sometimes, literally, three boxes of Sno-Caps and three Sprites, each for sale for fifty cents? It closed. It's gone. I don't want to dig any deeper. I value my life. I walked away from you, Four Star, but not before seeing a print of *Gone with the Wind* so perfect it felt like a massive hallucination from another dimension, where humans more operatic than us found a way to make the South's defeat in the Civil War the sexiest calamity that ever crashed into history.

But despite all of my film-junkie wanderings, the New Beverly was home base. And that night was a rarity for me. *One* movie, not the double feature I usually gobbled down. Just one film, complete immersion, and as much burning into memory as I could manage.

Because now, a year and five months after moving to Los Angeles, I'd found another competitor for my evenings. In fact, much like the other rep theaters that occasionally drew me from the New Beverly's punishing seats,

---

*It was always weirdly comforting to hear the female voice on their in-house trailers put that Britpop, lilting rise on the last syllable of *theatre*.

it was a host of lesser Night Cafés, enticing me toward the next big one, the next Room I Would Enter and Not Leave the Same.

After that first week, in 1995, of doing no stand-up—of getting my staff-writer sea legs and taking my first nibble at film freakdom, a gnashing, celluloid-crammed swallow—I'd roared back into my routine of going onstage as much as I could. If gluttony was the way I was going to learn filmmaking, I thought, then that was how I was going to keep my comedian muscles limber and lethal. As much stage time as possible. It was the only way I knew.

So this was my routine, that first year:

1) Wake up in my blank, Ikea-heavy apartment on Normandie. 2) Drive to work at Ren-Mar studios. 3) Carb-and-coffee-heavy breakfast at craft services. 4) Pitch sketches. 5) Play *Doom* and *Hexen* at my computer for most of the day, then hastily write whatever sketches they accepted twenty minutes before they were due. 6) Self-righteously piss and moan about the legitimate notes and concerns the producers had with my sloppy, poorly executed concepts. I mean, couldn't they see how *brilliant* my idea was? Who cared about the typos or the fact that the sketch might not really have an ending? Ambiguity is what classic cinema and memorable sketch comedy are all about, *maaaaaaaaaan.*

At least I've kept the painful memory of every self-serving, lazy argument I made while I was at *MADtv*, to remind me to work on the execution as hard as the conception hit me. But that's another book.

Because my other routine—my lunar routine, my nocturnal gauntlet—was this:

1) Wet my hair, wash my face, brush my teeth in the men's room at Ren-Mar around seven thirty, which is usually when my day ended unless it was a Friday night taping. 2) Grab dinner. Two plastic trays of sushi from Ralph's and a big Evian was a reliable favorite. I could eat it in my car without spilling anything on my shirt as I drove to either 3a) the New Beverly, or some other rep theater to catch a movie, or 3b) a comedy stage, somewhere.

But a new wrinkle had been thrown into my routine. An insane one, a magical-thinking one, a baseball-player-wearing-the-same-pair-of-socks-through-a-pennant-series superstitious one.

Remember how, after that first double feature at the New Beverly, I went back to my apartment and checked off—in my *Film Noir Encyclopedia* and first volume of *Cult Movies* and *The Psychotronic Encyclopedia*—the date and place that I'd actually seen those movies? Well, I went and did it again with *The Nutty Professor* and then, a week later, with *Touch of Evil* and *Kiss of Death* (June 7 and 8, respectively, at the New Beverly).

And in *between* all of that—in between the Billy Wilder double feature and *The Nutty Professor* and then the two classic film noirs, I did a set at the UnCabaret at Luna Park.

The UnCabaret was a Sunday night show started by Beth Lapides in 1993 as an alternative to a lot of the mainstream clubs in Los Angeles. Enough has been written about it elsewhere, so let me boil it down here: Lapides's creation was a crucial offshoot of spaces like the Holy City Zoo and, by the time I started doing sets there in 1994, one of the best places for a comedian to get seen, advance their career, gain new followers and grow beyond their limits.

It was also nerve-wracking, going in there to do sets. I was suddenly sharing the stage with idols of mine, like David Cross, Dana Gould and Laura Kightlinger. And the crowd was packed with not only rabid comedy fans but celebrities who were even bigger idols to me. I descended the stairs one night to do my set and realized, in an ass-clinching moment after I'd passed them, that the goddamned motherfucking oh-my-fucking-Christ *Beastie Boys* were the three guys I'd pushed past to make my way to the stage.

I had a great set that night. Killer. I'd only rarely connected like that with an audience, making even my moments of silence and fumbling into laughs. And in front of the guys who crafted *Paul's Boutique*, a hip-hop album as dense as one of Gabriel García Márquez's phantasmal libraries!

Where *did* that sudden surge come from? Why did I suddenly feel like I had a nitrous tank strapped to a part of me, like Mad Max's V8 Interceptor in *The Road Warrior*?

Maybe, I thought, back in my apartment that night, it was the Five Books. The checking off of classic films, after actually going to watch them on-screen. As I filled in each hole in my movie buff's incomplete knowledge, perhaps I was unlocking some secret level of skill I had as a comedian.

Before you start in on me, yes, I realize now this was superstition and ritual and illogical voodoo-mind. Salt tossed over your shoulder. Always saying "the Scottish play" and not . . . you know. Hats on beds.

Movies checked off in books. That was to become my ritual. My secret spell, my wards and glyphs and incantations, aiding me in my pursuit as a comedian. And—I seemed to keep forgetting—my goal to become a filmmaker. That would happen, right?

So after that night at the UnCabaret, I wasn't merely going out to see movies. I was seeking magical assistance. Anywhere I could find it, often at the risk of career, life or relationships. A late matinee of *Last Tango in Paris* (*Cult Movies*, volume 2) on a Sunday in San Francisco, which made me almost miss getting to my show at Cobb's that evening. *Bloodsucking Freaks* (*The Psychotronic Encyclopedia*) at midnight at the Sunset 5, sneaking out of an amazing rooftop party downtown and racing across the city to make it on time. If I missed even a *second* of the film, it didn't count. I was an obsessive sorcerer with a jealous, sentient spellbook.

Jesus—oh God, I'm just now remembering this; holy moley was I an asshole—I even made a girl I'd been going out with for six years walk to her car *by herself* at two o'clock in the morning because I was in the middle of an all-night horror-thon at the Cinerama Dome. *I Married a Monster from Outer Space* had just ended, and *Mr. Sardonicus* was about to start.

"So, I'm really going to walk out there, two in the morning, by myself? You're okay with that?" I can still see her half-exasperated, half-pitying face in the semi-darkness.

"Well, I've never, uh, seen the . . . uh . . . the beginning of . . ."

She justifiably broke up with me shortly after that.

So that was my push-pull, that first year as a sprocket fiend and born-again stage ghoul, all through the rest of 1995 and into 1996. Devouring movies, checking off, and convincing myself that my improving fortunes onstage came from expanding this alternate movie world inside my head.

I did something that night, watching *Beauty and the Beast* (listed in both *The Psychotronic Encyclopedia* and *Cult Movies* volume 1—bonus!), that I'd only done rarely up to that point. I tried to think about what the actors and directors had gone through to make it. I'd read about that movie, knew the struggle that Cocteau had, what with the postwar shortages in film stock at the time. And poor Jean Marais, his skin cracked and burning from the animal fur glued to it for five hours every morning. Cocteau himself, his stress and inner turmoil erupting onto his skin, checking into a hospital and turning the reins of his masterpiece over to another director. These people had struggled against even more than the usual odds against making a movie.* They'd done it in spite of the

---

*And I was still two years away from seeing *Les Enfants du Paradis*—for which I took a punishing early flight back from the Toronto Sketch Comedy Festival so I'd land in Los Angeles in time to get to the New Beverly to see it.

hostility of the world to the mere act of filmmaking, the indifference of the public to gauzy fantasy in the face of exhausted, war-ravaged reality.

I'd think of *Beauty and the Beast* every time I'd do a set in some small, out-of-the-way coffeehouse, often one I'd booked myself or helped promote with my friends. A lot of times we'd end up performing for each other. I did an afternoon at Highland Grounds—me and Sarah Silverman and Tenacious D—in front of fifteen people, half of whom slammed their laptops shut or scooped up their coffee and scones to find a quieter place away from these *fucking clowns*. I'd do the tiny, stark, overlit Onyx Café on Vermont, milling around with three or four other comedians while a pre–"Loser" Beck would pack up his guitar and his audience of eight would head for the door. The Creativity Bookstore, out at the beach, a usually empty space with the occasional tanned, gorgeous homeless guy and his dog.*

---

*I don't know where else to put this story, but it needs to be told.

One night, at the Onyx, a bunch of us were doing sets. I remember Bobcat Goldthwait being there, and Greg Behrendt, and Laura Kightlinger, and a few others. We were, essentially, performing for each other. The Onyx was a white, featureless space with harsh lighting and a big picture window that opened up out to Vermont. Passersby could peer inside and see a life-sized terrarium of a poorly attended open mike.

Halfway through the show, an older, African American man came in and sat down in one of the white plastic folding chairs. The chairs were in a sloppy half-circle around the "stage," which was really just a space on the floor with a microphone in a stand. I think Laura was onstage when this happened.

Laura finished her set. We laughed and applauded—all eight of us. The older, African American man slowly raised his hand. The emcee, midway through introducing the next act, stopped and said, "Sir? You have a comment?"

The show at the Onyx Café moved across the street to Pedro's Grille, and as 1995 turned to 1996, it caught on. Bigger crowds, bigger comedians—Bobcat Goldthwait and Jon Stewart would drop in. Something was beginning to gel. No one could say what it was, exactly, but my group of friends were starting to come into their own. Tenacious D and *Mr. Show* came out of the Diamond Club—another usually half-empty showcase theater, on Hollywood Boulevard. Stand-up comedians mixed with characters and sketches. Will Ferrell performed with his group Simpatico. Jeff Hatz staged his elaborate "Assembly North Gym," a brilliant mock-up of a high school assembly, with various comedians exorcising whatever angst they carried from teachers, administrators, or dismissive fellow students.

Then Margaret Cho got a sitcom. Jack Black became a movie star. Was it our time? I remember watching *Psych-Out* and *The Trip* and *Head* at the New Beverly, seeing Jack Nicholson and Dennis Hopper getting to act in movies only because they also wrote and produced them. Me

---

The man said, "Yes. I want to get sober, too."

Everyone was silent. The emcee's mouth dropped half-open but he didn't say anything.

"I need to get sober," said the man. More silence.

Then the older man laughed and said, "If that's how it is then fuck y'all. I knew this was a scam."

And then he rose, dignified, from his chair and strode out into the night.

It took a few more seconds of silence and then Bobcat said, "Oh Jesus, he thought this was an AA meeting. And we didn't help him."

A couple of us ran out onto Vermont, trying to catch him, maybe lead him to some help with his drinking. But he'd vanished. Probably to a bar, for some righteous drinking.

Comedy!

and my friends got to go onstage only because we asked a bookstore or coffee shop manager to let us do a show. Then *Easy Rider* came along and pulled Nicholson and Hopper and, if they were close enough to their jetwash, everyone else in their crew into the establishment.

And then came the Largo.

The Largo had opened in August of 1996—formerly a dodgy, mocking attempt at a French bistro called the Café Largo. An Irish music promoter named Mark Flanagan had bought the place, planning on showcasing the music acts he liked, in the fashion he thought they should be seen. Like Sherman over at the New Beverly with his idiosyncratic pairing of movies, Flanagan saw connective tissue between, say, Aimee Mann and Colin Hay and an audience that might actually like to sit down and relax with a glass of wine and let the musicians take their time. A relief from the knee-and-eardrum-destroying, standing-room-only rock club model. The way the New Beverly was a relief from the multiplex. There were plenty of multiplexes in L.A. in which to see *Con Air* or *Broken Arrow** or Eddie Murphy's remake of *The Nutty Pro-*

---

*Was there some sort of secret rivalry between *Broken Arrow* and *Con Air*? *Broken Arrow* came out in the winter of 1996 and climaxes with one of the craziest over-the-top, Wile E. Coyote villain deaths I'd seen up to that point (John Travolta speared and launched through a train by his own stolen, deactivated nuclear missile). Next summer here comes *Con Air*, which ends with John Malkovich leg-speared, dropped from a ladder and then head-smooshed by an industrial press—while lying on a conveyor belt. In 1998 there was *Armageddon*, and Bruce Willis nuking himself on a killer asteroid after experiencing a video montage of Liv Tyler, but it wasn't the topper I was expecting. If only *Shakespeare in Love* had ended with Joseph Fiennes falling off a cliff wearing rocket skates . . .

fessor. Nothing wrong with those movies. If people need bread and circuses, better it be bread from the best flour and springwater, and circuses under the cleanest canvas tents with the healthiest animals. Also nothing wrong with standing crotch-to-ass in a screaming throng while a band sends sonic boulders of aggression out of monolith speakers and blasts the dust off your skin. Regular doses of Spectacle and Subtle enhance your life.

Flanagan wanted to bring some Subtle. Once he bought the place he tried to change its name to the Establishment, after Peter Cook's London club in the sixties, where Marty Feldman and the Goons and eventually Monty Python sprung from. But the previous owners, for murky legal reasons, had a say in the matter. And they said no. So Flanagan said fuck it and just changed its name to the Largo.

It wasn't long before Flanagan got the idea to make Monday night a comedy night. Or maybe it wasn't his idea—maybe he was approached by Josh di Donato, who'd started the Onyx show and taken it to Pedro's and now, with a rabid weekly audience, was looking for a nicer venue.*

---

*Josh di Donato is another story, and it'd be cruel and insensitive of me to say anything too harsh about the poor bastard in these pages. That's why we're crouching down in this footnote while I whisper to you. Look, yeah, he was kind of fucked up. I've run into him recently and he's a much calmer, more self-effacing guy. Without going into too much detail, he knew how to book a room. He was a one-man Internet mailing list before the Internet became the all-reaching clarion it is today. Tireless promoter. But also, tragically, a frustrated comedian who thought of himself as equal to a lot of the performers he booked. It's forgivable—as you'll see, when you read the rest of this chapter, we were all fucked up and full of ourselves then. There was a madness to the Largo, and Josh, just as much as anyone else, got caught up in

What mattered to me, and to every other comedian who started doing those Monday nights, was that, even more than the UnCabaret, the Largo was truly a place to change your career. A good set could literally change the path of your life. I walked back into the kitchen one night, and there was Paul Thomas Anderson, inviting me to be in *Magnolia*. Another night the Farrelly brothers came, and I started punching up their movies.

And that was just me. There were suddenly other faces, other amazing talents. Paul F. Tompkins, dapper and razor witted, who, on most Mondays, did what another comedian described to me as "structural damage" to the room. Here came people I remembered from San Francisco—Greg Behrendt, Greg Proops, Karen Kilgariff. Mary Lynn Rajskub, whom I'd first seen in San Francisco doing poetry at the Albion, was now bringing the same off inflection, broken iambic attack and startling shifts up onto the stage. The Largo audience went anywhere, shifted gears effortlessly. None of us had ever seen anything like it. Sarah Silverman, David Cross and Louis CK would go up and destroy like they were playing the video game *Doom* in "God mode."* Zach Galifianakis would

---

it. That's another book—and not mine to write. Also, Pedro's Grille became even shadier and scarier than the Four Star, so it followed that Josh would want to take his admittedly superlative show to a more stable room. He'd have been a conquering hero if he'd just stuck to booking the room. But he let his hubris lead him up onto the stage, and so now he's an older, wiser motherfucker with a rueful calm. I like him. I do.

*"God mode": endless ammo, endless lives. A lot of my *MADtv* sketches never got written because I was too busy mowing down Beholders and Cacodemons with a pulse rifle.

be up there, be-scarved and banging on a piano, peppering the silences with surreal one-liners. Mitch Hedberg went on one night and, in the middle of a set of even more surreal one-liners, said one of the wisest and truest things I've ever heard about comedy, and especially about a comedian's hubris: "Beware of any comedian who writes for half an hour and then tells you they have thirty minutes of new material."

But that was the lure and danger of the Largo. You could go onstage totally unprepared, and if the crowd was in the right mood, you could actually do a solid half hour of off-the-top-of-your-head material that would vibrate the walls and lift you into an ego cloud you had no business floating in.

That was what Monday nights at the Largo were. And for the first time, the outside world started to notice. *Spin* magazine, *Rolling Stone*, *Vanity Fair*—journalists were starting to write about it. Casting people and directors and producers would come to the shows. Again—and in opposition to everything I'd ever learned about being a comedian and everything I say now when giving advice— you could change your career with a single set.

And keep in mind, for the most part, you *can't* change your career with a single set. Can't do it. Don't try. Get that thought out of your head, now. The ones who make it, I still say, are the ones who go up, night after night, honing their craft, focusing more on the moment and blah blah blah. But there's a gigantic exception to that rule, and it's an exception that comes when time, place and venue line up. That convergence doesn't last long, but when it happens, the "you can't change your career with one set" rule goes right out the window.

It's happened before. *The Ed Sullivan Show. The Tonight Show*—if Carson called you over to the couch after your set. The Comedy Store in the early eighties, I suppose. It's happened for other creative professions as well. The Grand Ole Opry. CBGB.

And it happened, for a time, at the Largo. And when it did, we started to eat each other alive.

Never in overt ways. More subtle, seventh-grade-cafeteria-pecking-order ways. Like jostling for the closing spot 'cause you were the alpha and believed no one could follow you. Or hanging out every single Monday, even if you weren't booked, on the off chance someone wouldn't show and you'd go up in their place. Comedians, addicted to the crack cocaine response of the Largo audience, would wear out their welcome, either in terms of multiple Monday nights in a row or, once they got onstage, hogging time. Twenty-minute closing sets became half hours became forty-five minutes. I know this because I was one of the worst offenders.

Sometimes I'd be in the room when someone—a friend, a fucking *friend*—would go onstage and I'd leave, not wanting to see them kill, not liking the curdled butane stink it'd create in my stomach, watching it. I remember one comedian, another San Francisco transplant who ended up spurning the stage for staff writing, strutting around one Monday night after looking at the lineup. "They've got me going on last. My first time visiting here, and they've got me going on last," he said with the worst mock humility

I've ever seen. Turns out his name was simply at the top of the *comp* list, which made it appear that he was closing. His name had been jotted down on the lineup *after* the headliner's name, as a note to the doorman. He convinced himself, for the twenty minutes before someone took him aside and explained the confusion (after which point he fled in embarrassment), that just by *appearing* in the room, he had been given the prime spot in the lineup. He wasn't even on the show. Good thing, too—he would have had to follow Todd Glass, who was (and remains) a force of nature. Still, I envied his confidence and delusion.

That was the effect the Largo—which, at that point, had become industry shorthand for "the alternative elite"—had on a comedian visiting it for the *first time*. Imagine what it was doing to all of us—the core group who were there every single Monday. We were glowing and crackling with ambition, with the sick radiation of potential fame and riches, swelling and mutating, terminal.

Other comedians divided off into cliques, treating friends, suddenly, like outsiders. A lot of these cliques were held together only by the energy created from excluding everyone. Once everyone was excluded, they'd turn on each other, and weeks later the members of the clique were enemies. And no, I'm not writing this to name names, settle scores, plant gossip. I was just as bad— if not worse—in my behavior and greed as anyone I'm describing. They've all got their stories to tell and I'm sure books will be written, blogs will be posted. The names, alliances and enmities don't matter. Not to me. It only matters that we were young, and we each handled fame (or the promise of it) and success (or the hint of it) in our own, unique, clumsy and terrible ways. And what *also* matters, in my wider memory, is seeing firsthand what I'd only read about in places like Warhol's Factory, and Studio 54, and the Algonquin Round Table before that. Did even Ben Franklin think that life was some transitory, nebulous clique? "I must soon quit this scene . . ." And he would have been saying that to George Washington, who, if he wasn't the Andy Warhol of the Founding Fathers, certainly shared his hairstyle.

Oh, and here's something else that would happen, every few Mondays. See, once the Largo had been mentioned in, say, *Rolling Stone*? Suddenly we had big-time, mainstream headliners dropping by, wanting to flex their egos, roll with the new, and deny aging and death.*

These sets rarely went well. As one of the Largo regulars pointed out, onstage one Monday after a previous week's painful sitcom-titan flameout, "Is there anything more entertaining than watching some huge headliner come up here and eat it? And then attack the crowd for eating it? Nervously laughing while saying, 'Well, I guess this alternative comedy is all about *not* getting laughs, right? Heh heh heh.' *Sweat sweat sweat.*"

He was right. But the flip side of what he said was *also* true. The Largo, as amazing and nurturing as it was for the musicians and comedians who played there, could be

---

*No, I'm not going to name any names here, either. Especially 'cause I suspect, in another ten years, I'm going to be dropping by whatever 2024's version of the Largo is to tell myself that my aching feet and spasming back are in no way signs of my unavoidable disintegration.

just as deadly and reality-warped as the castle of wonders and horrors in Cocteau's *Beauty and the Beast*. Because as entertaining as watching a mainstream comedian crash and burn in the Largo was, it was equally as hilarious watching a Largo hothouse flower wither and die in the harsher air of a mainstream club or, worse, on the road. "I went to Blockbuster with my friend *Terry*, right? And, so, he rents *The Pelican Brief*, can you believe it? I mean, uh . . . I mean, if you *knew* Terry. I guess . . . oh shit, you guys don't know Terry. Great." No, they didn't. Nor did they know the significance of referencing Kim Deal or *The Fast Show* or, as I discovered one night at the Riviera in Las Vegas, movie director Sam Fuller.*

It went back to Hedberg's warning, back to Cocteau's castle. Inside the Largo, especially during its heyday, we were all kings and rebels and artists forging the new, and emerging victorious from the jungle every single time. Outside of the Largo? Just like Warhol's Factory denizens outside of their silver-wallpapered paradise, or Dorothy Parker away from her chair and vodka at the Algonquin, we were still comedians, blinking in the daylight, schlepping onto planes, nervous at auditions. For as much as we made fun of mainstream hack comedians, with their bits about airline food and cats vs. dogs? Alternative comedy soon had its own hack premises. The Shitty Blockbuster Movie We Still Shelled Out Money to See and Were Now Lambasting. The Audition That Didn't Go Well. The

---

*That was during a bit where I suggested that *Forrest Gump* might not be that good a film. An audience member politely pointed out, "It made a lotta money, you asshole!"

Looking at Our Notes While Working on the Idea We Just Wrote Down and Were Trying to Work Out Onstage. Dozens of others.

I was right in the middle of this, by the way. My sets at the Largo were going great guns, and my road gigs— my headlining gigs, where I was actually making money (after *MADtv* decided to soldier on without me at the end of season two in 1997)—were starting to suffer. I was slow in realizing that a killer half an hour at the Largo meant about five solid, usable minutes on the road. Again, Mitch Hedberg's warning, unheeded.

On top of all this, I was falling deeper and deeper into my movie-watching-for-success-in-comedy superstition. I look back in my calendars and I'm amazed I didn't kill anyone, racing from some of these Monday night screenings to make it to the Largo. The New Beverly was always a godsend—a seven thirty screening of *The Pink Panther* or *Jason and the Argonauts* at the New Beverly meant a short drive down Beverly, a right onto Fairfax and then snag a parking space in the alley behind the Largo and zip through the kitchen with plenty of time to grab a drink, go over my notes, get a feel for the crowd and go onstage. Tales Café, just a little farther down La Brea from Beverly, was an equally short drive. I've done sets at the Largo with the image of James Coburn's paper-shredder grin from *The President's Analyst* in my head, or Jane Wyman's perky sneer from *Crime by Night*, after racing from Tales.

But other nights. Oh man. A restored print of *It's a Wonderful Life* at the Nuart, all the way out in Santa

Monica? How did I get through my set and *not* burst into tears, from the combination of both terror from the drive and emotion from the end of that film?

And even worse—one night I made it all the way from the Town Center 5 in Encino, fresh from a screening of *The Garden of the Finzi-Continis*,* and *still* made it to the Largo in time to do a set. I don't remember that set going well. Maybe I used up whatever luck I got from seeing de Sica's gorgeous memory box of a film in not dying while I slalomed and McQueen'd my way to another Monday night ego rub.

You see, the Largo was worth the risk. Because it completed an arc that started at Garvin's. Garvin's, back in DC in the summer of 1988, was a meat-and-potatoes vocational portal. This is stand-up comedy. You can either do it or not. If you show up every week, you'll get better. If you get better, you'll get work. Once you start getting work you need to figure out what will keep getting you work and craft your comedy along those lines.

Four years of that, of solidly working the road, of trying to learn how to make any audience my audience. A lot of failures. A lot of triumphs. After a few years, I became bulletproof, as far as having to go up and win over any crowd with material that anyone could relate to, that the majority would recognize, be amused by and then forget

---

*Yes, it's a gorgeous film about a brief, elegiac time in Italy before the rise of the Nazis destroyed the fabulous, yet unrealistic, gated paradise of the Finzi-Continis. Sure there's a weak-ass parallel with me and my friends' immersing ourselves in the unreality of the Largo, but, I mean . . . *Nazis*. Nazis, right? There's no real comparison. That's why I'm hiding it down in this footnote.

the instant they left the club. I made myself bookable, competent and, ultimately, disposable.

Then came the Holy City Zoo. Pure innovation for innovation's sake. Risk taking in front of no one—or tiny crowds that would hone in on *you* and not the jokes you were telling. Suddenly I had to chew my way out of the safe, pastel cocoon of road material I'd built around myself and learn to walk the stage in the raw red of my exposed psyche, the deep blue of my lurking depression, the stinging white of my angers and resentments, the blazing yellow of my cowardice and the black black black of whatever dark thoughts I might be having. The Zoo was a flight simulator—where it was safe to see what it felt like to nose-turf the 747 of your art and you could walk away unharmed. It wasn't going to launch you onto a TV or movie screen, but it would help you link up with comedians who would make you better at what you did—only because you had no choice. You either got better or they cast you out. Unlike the Garvin's comics, they weren't impressed with the work you were *getting*. They were impressed with the work you were *doing*.

And then, the Largo. Where, miraculously, those two ideas—art and commerce, risk and opportunity—fused and created a nameless new drug. It hung in the air, a narcotic vapor, and we all breathed it. It made all of us ambitious, competitive, resentful, jealous and, ultimately, more creative than we'd ever been before or since. At least, that's how it affected me.

I look again at my calendars from this time—the sets I did, the movies I saw. And it hits me—I can remember almost every detail of each night at the Largo. The other rooms, other dates? I did sets at the Improv and the Laugh Factory, as well as places with names I can barely remember. Book Grinders. Checca. The Upfront Theatre. Tempest. I mean, I went onstage at all of 'em. Told jokes. But I couldn't tell you with whom, or what I said, or what anyone else did.

At the same time, I was seeing every single movie I could. There they all are, noted in the calendar boxes, with the theater I saw them at. And not just classics at the New Beverly. I was going to see big-budget new releases, too. *Turbulence* at the Galaxy. *The Relic* at Mann's Chinese. *First Knight. Judge Dredd. Double Team. Volcano.*

I couldn't tell you anything about them.

But I remember the way Dennis Hopper said, "Hey, wait . . . ," to the spooky girl who *might* be a mermaid near the beginning of Curtis Harrington's *Night Tide*—the way he delivered the line with just the right blend of longing, madness and terror. Or Timothy Carey screaming, "Please . . . please . . . please . . . please . . . take my HAND!" in *The World's Greatest Sinner.* Every second of Laura Dern's brilliantly empty-headed performance in *Citizen Ruth.* Harry Morgan, far away from his kindly Colonel Sherman T. Potter persona, sliding the penknife under Richard Basehart's fingernail in *Outside the Wall.* And so many more—random moments from small, brilliant, mostly forgotten films, which nevertheless burned their way into my memory better than anything the movie studios could attach sparklers and CGI to.

That's not to say that I thought all big-budget Hollywood movies were forgettable garbage and that true cinema was to be found solely in tiny, out-of-the-way indies. As the nineties approached the aughts, independent film began to fall victim to the same clichés I was seeing in alternative comedy. One night, after leaving a particularly precious slice of manufactured quirkiness at the Sunset 5, a screenwriter friend of mine said, "Jesus, are there only three plots of independent films? 'Oh no, we ripped off the mob,' 'Hitman on his last job,' and 'How do we get rid of this dead body?'"

He wasn't wrong. And the makers of *Anaconda* weren't wrong to let Jon Voight blaze all over creation with his seven-headed hydra of an accent, or to shoot his death by anaconda from the POV of the anaconda's stomach as its mouth opened, or have his corpse wink after it regurgitated him to make room for the even-more-delectable Jennifer Lopez. And Samuel L. Jackson's interrupted monologue in the middle of *Deep Blue Sea*? The audience in the Cinerama Dome *stood and cheered*—I swear to you—when the scene met its bloody, eviscerating conclusion.

It took me a few years, though—and a lot of nights at the Largo and a lot more nights in movie theater seats—before I learned that just because something was "indie" and "underground" didn't automatically give it value. I also had to learn to look for the moments of substance and impact in the everyday. I was sitting in a minimall Subway having a sandwich one evening, on my way from work to go to the Largo, when I read a quote by Italo Calvino: "seek and learn to recognize who and what, in the midst of inferno, are not inferno, then make them endure, give them space."

When I got to the Largo, there was a comedian onstage, literally reading a list of things he hated. That was it. No bigger jokes, no deeper insights, no startling twist. Just a list of things he didn't like. And he killed. That's when I began to suspect that maybe even the Largo had elements to it that were inferno.

I also learned, on Thursday, October 2, 1997, that a place that was, in itself, entirely inferno had bits worth saving.* That was my debut set at the Comedy Store. I was scheduled to film my first HBO comedy special in just over two weeks, up in San Francisco. Mitzi Shore, the owner of the Comedy Store, had heard tell of this. She called my manager and wanted to see a set from me.

The Comedy Store was, to me, a legendary stage with a lot of history. I was excited to do it. I was also very excited about where my career was going. HBO special, regular at this hot new room called the Largo. Things

---

*Davey Marlin-Jones. He was a film critic for the local CBS affiliate in Washington, DC, when I was growing up. And he'd do these roundups of currently playing movies, and he'd review them by taking out a stack of index cards, and depending on how he'd treat each card, that was how he felt about a movie. So for a movie like *They Call Me Bruce?* or *The Burning*, the card would get crumpled up and tossed over the news desk. The card for a film like *The Verdict* or *The Empire Strikes Back* would be lovingly slid into the inside pocket of his tweed jacket. But sometimes, he'd rip off a tiny corner of a card—a corner that would represent, say, Michael Moriarty's performance in *Q: The Winged Serpent* or Morgan Freeman's in *Street Smart*—and this little bit would be saved in his vest pocket before the rest of the card was flung away. Calvino's "inferno" principle, illustrated for me on the local news. Thanks, Davey. RIP.

were looking up. Time to do the Store. See what happened.

I got into the main room and Andrew "Dice" Clay was onstage. I'd been a huge fan of his when I was in college but I'd cooled a bit in my enthusiasm after I started doing comedy and began to think that what he did was becoming a bit repetitive and, after a while, slightly angry and resentful.

Well, he was spraying anger and resentment all over the room that night. Baiting the crowd, pissed off and seemingly entitled. I instinctively tuned him out as I made my way toward a dark table in the back, to go over my notes and get ready. And then . . .

. . . I tuned back in. Dice was, more than any comedian I'd seen at the Largo in the past few months up to that point, truly flying without a script. He segued from chatting amiably with a young wannabe actress in the front row to one of the most offensive, venomous, hilarious screeds about what, exactly, the phrase "follow your dreams" meant, especially in terms of Hollywood and the entertainment business. It involved, at various points, being the prettiest one in Omaha, tucking genitals under one's ass, and Marilyn Monroe. It was childish, profane and 100 percent true.

He left the stage and the room. I was genuinely, delightfully shaken up. I'd just seen a comedian—a comedian that, I'll admit, I and a lot of my Largo colleagues would regularly mock—deliver one of the more memorable sets I'd seen in a long time. On a random, rainy Thursday night in Los Angeles, to maybe one hundred people.

A few more comedians went up, and then me. I only had to do seven minutes. I did the newer stuff that I knew worked, that killed at the Largo as well as on the road. The set went great. The emcee brought me off. I walked away from the stage and there, sitting at the end of the aisle, like a soft, slumping Buddha, was Mitzi.

She extended her hand. I shook it. Cold vinyl.

She said, "Do you live in the city?"

"Yeah," I answered.

"Do you want to work as a doorman here?"

It took me a second to realize what she'd asked me. I recovered and said, "Well, I mean . . . I tour all the time, and in two weeks I'm filming my first—"

She whipped her hand away. She was still looking at me, but in a way that told me I was no longer in view. I trudged away, devastated. I thought my set went well.

There was a clutch of open-mikers, hanging at the back tables, waiting for their spot. A few of them came up to me.

"What'd she say?" This was from a comedian who was older than me, dressed in the height of comedian fashion, if it were 1984.

"She said I could work as a doorman here," I said. My tone must have sounded like the whine a balloon makes when it deflates.

The comedian's eyes went wide. "She *never* offers people the doorman spot on their first set!"

I suddenly saw the group of open-mikers not as a bunch of comedians, but as the doomed, alternate set of survivors in *The Poseidon Adventure*—the ones walking the wrong way, deeper into the sinking ship, exhorting Gene Hackman to follow them, insisting that *he's* the one going the wrong way. I had to get out of there.

"Dice used to be the doorman here, too!" Another of the comedians spat this at me as I pushed through the glass door, as if I were making a career-killing mistake.

That's the moment the Largo truly became a Night Café for me—when I realized that the extreme perfection of the Largo was, for me as a comedian, as dangerous as the extreme shittiness of the Comedy Store was for the clutch of open-mikers huddled in the back of its black-on-black-on-black, haunted* showroom. I saw the two choices in front of me, out on the Sunset Strip sidewalk, as I walked back to my car. Stay exclusive to the Largo and a hundred other alternative comedy rooms all over the city, and turn into a hothouse flower that could only perform in front of crowds that were *just so.* Or *only* do the mainstream rooms, and toughen my hide, and have my moments of humanity and transcendence leak through my pores randomly, the way Dice had just done, on weeknights when I wasn't getting paid, wasn't winning over new fans, was sweating resentment with the honesty.

I look at my calendars from after that night, as 1997 wound to a close and 1998 started up, and there it was— my solution. Still did Monday nights at the Largo—and

---

*The Comedy Store was Ciro's back in the forties. People murdered and disposed of in its back rooms, it was rumored. Lead-lined, bulletproof walls. Mickey Cohen himself survived a drive-by machine gun hit out front because he stooped down to pick up a dropped dollar. I don't believe in ghosts, but I do believe in vibes. And the Comedy Store has cosmically bad ones, to this day.

other nights, opening for Aimee Mann and Michael Penn's Acoustic Vaudeville shows. Opening for Tenacious D. And Colin Hay. And 2 Headed Dog. And *White Trash Wins Lotto*. And the Naked Trucker and T-Bones and a dozen of the other precious, unforgettable, near-perfect evenings that transpired in the Cocteau/*Beauty and the Beast* fortress of the Largo. The other comedians were still there, but the alliances and enmities weren't as strong. It felt like we'd all graduated high school and were looking back at some of the more passionate couplings and ruptures with the amusement and discomfort that you get flipping through an old yearbook. I hated *that* guy so much I wished him dead? *She* broke my heart? Wow.

One night Paul F. Tompkins and I found ourselves at the bar. We'd had our share of tension and competition and passive-aggressive jousting. I said something about how now most of us finished our set and either watched the rest of the show, contentedly, or simply left.

Paul took a gentlemanly sip of scotch and said, "Well, we all got to know each other, didn't we?"

A perfect song lyric as elegy, smuggled into conversation.

But as much as I still loved the Largo, I made it a point to go out on the road—to the less receptive cities, where I still had to win people over. And I made sure to do a night at the Improv—where I could still count on having a shitty set once in a while. Or the Laugh Factory, where I first auditioned for *Late Night with Conan O'Brien*, on a weekday "Latino Comedy Riot." Carlos Mencia was emceeing and brought me up by saying, verbatim,

"Okay, this next comedian's a white guy, but [over the rising boos] *give him a chance, motherfuckers*!" I didn't get booked on *Late Night* 'til years later. Looking back, I appreciate the struggle.

The Largo moved locations in 2008. Now it's in the much bigger, much grander Coronet. The Coronet is haunted by even more history than the Comedy Store could ever dream of. I still do shows at the new Largo at least once every two months. I'll never give up the nirvana of that stage or that crowd. But I've made it sweeter by always making sure that when I step foot onto it, I'm shaking off a weekend on the road or a night in front of cranky tourists at the Improv. I saw too many comedians acclimate to the Largo, to the point where any other environment shredded them like a Chihuahua in a dogfighting pit.

Even Cocteau's impossible castle, glowing up on the New Beverly screen, was a place that needed to be left behind before it had any value. The Largo was the only Night Café that changed me after I left but was still there for me to return to when I needed it. Besides, I was finally starting to take my first baby steps toward making films. Not as a director, mind you. It was as an actor—an extra, really—but that was a start, wasn't it?

Sure it was. Here, I'll show you.

CHAPTER FOUR

No Small Actors

Down Periscope, 1995

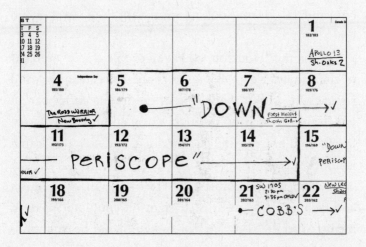

I was sitting in a multiplex in Sherman Oaks, nearly rising out of my seat, electrified with inspiration. Clint Howard had just spoken on-screen. It was a "Eureka!" moment for me.

It was Saturday, July 1, 1995. A pitiless hell-blast of an afternoon in the Valley. This wasn't the pleasant May warmth of the Saturday I'd first entered the New Beverly, two months before. The Valley in July was a concentrated slice of the sun. Everyone on the sidewalk was a scuttling ant under a magnifying glass. I'd tucked myself into the cool-and-carpeting oasis of the Sherman Oaks Galleria, into their bland multiplex, to see Ron Howard's *Apollo 13*.

I was digging it. I'm a sucker for contemporary history, especially when it involves uncomfortable-looking clothing, galactic risk undertaken with slide-rule-level technology, and Ed Harris looking grim. *Apollo 13* was a fun lunch.

I was at the "Houston, we have a problem . . . ," moment in the movie. Kevin Bacon stirs the oxygen tanks, and somewhere within the wiring of the fragile coffee can in which they're soaring through space, an imp leaps loose. Sparks and fire, rattling and lurching, and now the drama is under way.

Back at ground control, Ed Harris's team of scientists and technicians gape at their eight-bit computer screens, seeing Atari 2600–style error messages and hearing ominous, urgent bleeps. These are men who, like Keanu Reeves in *The Matrix* or a hedge fund risk manager, could see danger in tumbling clusters of numbers. The numbers here add up to defeat and death for the three astronauts.

And there's Clint Howard, wearing a pair of glasses that would soon adorn the bridge of every hipster's nose in Williamsburg and Los Feliz. And a tight, conservative comb-over haircut and Church of the SubGenius pipe. He's one voice in a chorus of calm, robotic engineer and monitor vigil keepers, spitting out only what the numbers could prove.

And he does it, too. At first. Reading off of his frantic,

scrambled screen, in defiance of its digital panic, he says, tersely but professionally, "O_2 tank two not reading at all. Tank one is at seven hundred twenty-five PSI and falling. Fuel cells one and three are, uh . . ."

And then a pause. He's *so* determined, in that moment, to offer up his report, to be a part of the team, to *function*.

But that *pause*. It's as long as an intake of breath. And then, with a frightened flutter in his voice (and notice how there's also a touch of anger, at himself, for allowing this moment of doubt in the face of science and the infinite):

"Oh boy, *what's* going on here?"

That single moment in *Apollo 13*, that single line reading by a lifer actor who, like the character he's playing, never fails to show up and deliver a solid piece of work, pierced me. I realized that up until that point in *Apollo 13*, all of its pyrotechnic special effects and thrilling cinematography had left me cold. Well, not cold. I liked the rocket taking off and the explosions and the editing and the *Apollo 13* itself spinning through the void, spitting instantly frozen oxygen. Good moviemaking.

But it was Clint Howard's line. The pause, and the "oh boy," which hit me with twice the impact of a thousand rocket engines and all of their vulcanized thrust.

I'd seen single lines in movies land with that kind of weight before, at least for me. Jerry Ziesmer, as "Jerry the Civilian" in *Apocalypse Now*, intoning the icy line "Terminate . . . with extreme prejudice." The single, terminal "Neutered," from *Gates of Heaven*. Glenn Shadix's "ES-kimo" from *Heathers*. "Rosebud," fer Chrissakes.

Up until this moment, in my sealed, air-conditioned

cube in a Sherman Oaks multiplex, I'd always noted those moments and enjoyed them and then lost them to the larger flow (or failure) of whatever movie I was watching. They were either a tiny, perfected detail in a larger masterpiece or a brief glimmer of goodness in something forgettable. Like a fast food meal where, out of nowhere, you pluck one of the most transcendentally perfect French fries out of a soggy mound of blandness.

But things were different now. Because now, watching *Apollo 13*, I was halfway through filming my first movie role.

I'd been cast in a movie called *Down Periscope*. Kelsey Grammar was playing an iconoclastic, brilliant submarine captain with a tattoo on his dick. He gets picked to helm an old diesel sub in a war game to see if a rattletrap relic from World War II, in the hands of radical terrorists, could be used successfully in a suicide attack.* The crew he's tasked to work with are the usual misfits, malcontents, rogues and oddballs that are usually assembled around whatever comedic alpha dog drives movies like this. His rivals in the exercise, arrayed against him in a sleek nuclear submarine, are William H. Macy and Bruce Dern. Rip Torn is his only ally among the top brass. Somewhere within the bowels of Kelsey's sub lurks Harry Dean Stanton, as a crusty old engineer. In terms of my sprocket-fiend tastes, *Down Periscope* was a smorgasbord.

I didn't get to meet any of those guys, by the way.

---

*Oh man. This was six years before the September 11 attacks. I hope this film doesn't become prophecy.

I'd been cast as "*Stingray* Radioman," the nameless sailor assigned to sit at and monitor the radio of the *Stingray*, the diesel sub. I'd lurk in the background, silently taking in numbers and facts. And, at one point in the script, I look up from my station and say to Kelsey, "Radio message for you, sir. It's Admiral Graham."

Not an auspicious debut. It's not Sydney Greenstreet in *The Maltese Falcon* or Eddie Murphy in *48 Hrs.* or even Nick Nolte in *Dirty Little Billy*, whom I *still* can't spot after watching that muddy masterpiece three times. But it was work, and a SAG card, and getting used to the drudgery of acting in movies. Without having to expend any effort of my own—I'm sitting in every single scene except one, which we'll get to shortly—I was able to watch as Kelsey and the other actors did take after take, from angle after angle, to slowly assemble what would be scenes important, inconsequential and a combination of both. I sat at my fake radio inside a practical submarine set that had, according to one of the producers, also been used in *Run Silent, Run Deep* (was I sitting in a chair that once held the ass of Don Rickles?) and concluded that shooting a movie was like blasting a tunnel through a mountain. Or brushing every grain of sand off of a fossil. You attacked it relentlessly. The form was hidden in unyielding, indifferent rock. Or, in the case of a movie, nonjudgmental reels of virgin celluloid. It really came down to where you pointed the camera. And how you assembled the pieces afterward. I must have known that in the abstract, sitting in the New Beverly, marveling at the shower scene from *Psycho* or a Kurosawa katana fight, but this was the first time I'd seen the process from the "take one" point.

Our director was David S. Ward. He wrote *The Sting*! Won an Oscar for it! Then started directing. Now it was twenty-one years after his fingertips first touched the gold plating on an Oscar statuette. He was sitting in front of a half-submarine set, telling Rob Schneider to yell louder. And David wore the bemused, happy expression of a man who was truly fascinated and startled by where his journey was taking him. I missed noticing it until recollecting all of this, just now.

I sat in my chair in front of a fake radio, pretending the water I was sipping was bracing navy coffee. I sat there and thought about Big Hollywood Stars who'd started as background actors. Richard Dreyfuss's concerned face, poking out of the crowd of rooming house boarders near the end of *The Graduate*. Tony Curtis, silent but magnetic, sharing maybe three steps of a close dance with Yvonne De Carlo before Burt Lancaster sweeps her away, back into the main narrative of *Criss Cross*. Alan Ladd, in silhouette, at the end of *Citizen Kane*.

Were those guys, even then, working some inner engine, some focus-pulling voodoo that set them on the path to bigger roles? Not that I was even looking to become a lead actor like them. My thinking was to become a solid character actor, a working-all-the-time type like Buscemi or, deep in the fake engine room of the fake sub I was sitting in, Harry Dean Stanton. That's how I would observe every kilowatt, sprocket and tape measure of the filmmaking process, until I grew into the Great Director I was destined to be. I mean, John Ford was an extra in *The Birth of a Nation*.* Right?

I had a radio, a coffee cup and my profile to the camera for every single scene I was in. I had a single line of dialogue. For now, I had scene after scene in the background, blurred by the foreground antics of Harland Williams and Toby Huss and Schneider.

I sat there at my fake radio and thought of a story a stage actor friend of mine from New York had told me. Apocryphal, probably. But I was holding on to it like it was gospel, at least for the situation I was in now. Sanford Meisner, the legendary acting teacher, was doing a play early in his career. He was young and was just a background extra. A man sitting at a desk. While they were rehearsing the director suddenly singled Sanford out, yelled at him for pulling focus from the main actors. All Sanford was supposed to do was sit at a desk in the background and pretend to fill out forms while the drama happened in front of him. But the simple act of his writing on paper became more fascinating than anything the two leads could do with their pages and pages of dialogue.

"What are you doing back there?" asked the director.

Sanford said, "I'm trying to draw a perfect seven." Over and over, that's what Sanford tried to do. And his concentration on the task was so intent, so laser-hot, that it became the center of attention.

Could I do that with a hollow radio and a coffee cup? And if I did, wouldn't I *not* be doing the job I was hired

---

*A Klansman!

for? On the other hand, wasn't I supposed to think about, even at this near-faceless start of my movie career, learning how to hold an audience's attention on a movie screen? If this sounds grandiose, please remember that these are the thoughts that go through every extra's mind, in every TV show or movie or play you see. It's okay to have them.

But it wasn't smart, I soon learned, to act on them.

"What're you doing back there?" asked David on my second day of shooting. This was at the end of June, before we all took a break for the July 4 weekend.

I'd done something brilliant, I thought. I'd taken a sip of my coffee and reacted like it tasted god-awful, and did an exaggerated, almost silent-movie move of putting the cup back down, like it contained nitroglycerin that might explode if I set the cup down anything less than delicately.

"I just figured, you know, maybe the coffee tastes bad, and . . ."

David said, with zero malice, "You don't need to do that, Patton." He'd probably said this to a dozen different day players in a dozen different films by that point in his career. He'd seen the impulse before and understood where it came from, and he wasn't about to shame me for it. But seriously, Patton, sit in the fucking background. Don't act out the thirty-page character bio you've written in your head for "*Stingray* Radioman." You're not Jules in *Pulp Fiction*.

So that's how it went my first few days on *Down Periscope*. Fiddle with dials that did nothing, scrunch my eyes at the silence coming in on my radioman's headphones. Be a gray blur. This was my equivalent, acting-wise, of doing open mikes where I did seven minutes in front of three people at two o'clock in the morning. I was putting the time in. Good. I was happy to do it.

I was even happier to hang in between shots. Because the camera had to roam all around the inside of the submarines, there were stretches—hours and, sometimes, days—when I'd come in and the actors in my shot angles ended up sitting around outside their trailers. Card games, board games. Someone set up a weight bench. I'd sit and listen to Toby talk about nightmare construction jobs he'd done, or Harland would tell us about a series of children's books he was writing. *This is how it must be on movie sets*, I was thinking. You find creative ways to pass the time, and if it was with a group of people you liked, even better. There were mild, sunshiny days on the Fox lot while we waited. Ken Hudson Campbell, who played Buckman, the ship's cook whom Rob Schneider's character would yell at constantly, noticed there were a lot of studio golf carts sitting around, unused. The next day, without anyone saying anything to anyone, we all came in with newly purchased Super Soaker guns. Each of us would grab a golf cart—or pair up, with one driver and one shooter—and do an eight-mile-an-hour *Road Warrior* reenactment all over the studio lot. Until one day when we realized we'd slurped up every volt of charge in every single golf cart battery the studio had. Then we got shut down. Oh well. Back to Texas Hold'em with sunflower seeds for chips.

We made up sea chanteys. Invented card games with illogical rules. Challenged each other to see how much weight we could bench-press. Talked about frustrating auditions and crazy girlfriends and anything. Everyone was relaxed and enjoying each other's company and had their eyes on the long, colorful lifer's arc of working in show business. Everyone except for me, of course. Make no mistake—outwardly, I was jovial. Inwardly? I was a box of snakes. Being on a movie set dawn to dusk was making me miss movies at the New Beverly. Movies I could have been ritualistically checking off in one of my Five Books. This was the first of many ignored warnings (removing myself from parties and social interaction, losing a girlfriend, losing sleep, subsisting on a diet of theater snacks and soft drinks) that maybe my movie addiction needed to be handled and quelled rather than stoked.

Because despite all the fun I was having, I still finished that first week frustrated and impatient. This was my usual state of mind all through my twenties. Wasn't it everyone's? I wanted to headline comedy clubs. Wanted to get bigger roles as an actor. Wanted to write epic scripts and then direct them as world-changing movies. How in the fuck was that going to happen if I didn't make my first screen appearance somehow memorable?

Does anyone act more like an overserious senior citizen with time running out on their chance for immortality than someone in their twenties?

So I finished my first week of shooting *Down Periscope*, somehow ended up in the Valley, and plunked down to watch *Apollo 13*. And I left that screening with Clint Howard's line reading pinging around my skull and my path clear. I knew what I had to do.

"There's a call for you, sir. Admiral Graham."

There was a period at the end of each of those sentences. *That* was crucial. Here's why. Almost exactly one year before, I'd filmed my first-ever TV appearance. The "Couch" episode of *Seinfeld*. Jason Alexander is trying to rent *Breakfast at Tiffany's*, so he can avoid having to read the book for a book club he's joined. I play the video store clerk who tells him the movie's been rented. He asks if he can see who rented the movie. I say, "Sorry, sir. It doesn't work that way."

I was crashing at a house full of comedians at the time, for the week I was in Los Angeles auditioning. I was going over my sides for the part—when you're starting, a single-line day player part gets more scrutiny and sweat than Hickey's monologue at the end of *The Iceman Cometh*.

One of the comedians, a veteran of a punishing audition-a-day regimen that was just starting to pay off in day parts on sitcoms, told me, "See that period? Every period's the beginning of a new thought." I took that into my *Seinfeld* audition and got the part.

And now here I was, back on the *Down Periscope* set for my second week of filming. I'd written on the *MADtv* pilot two months earlier and they were waiting to hear whether or not they'd get picked up. For now, I was logically in the movie until the end—sitting in the background in the main cabin, which is where the bulk of the film's action took place. My background actor "ploy" of slinging a little over-the-top not-enjoying-my-coffee pantomime hadn't paid off. But I was fresh from seeing Clint Howard perfectly nail that scene in *Apollo 13* with his sublime line reading. And I'd remembered the "every period is a new thought" suggestion from my actor friend.

And this was the week I'd be filming my line.

"There's a call for you, sir. Admiral Graham."

I rolled those words around in my head. What new direction would I zing the line in after that period? Would I say, very matter-of-factly and professionally, that there was, indeed, a call coming in, and then drip a little acid onto the words *Admiral Graham*? Make it seem like I shared Kelsey's distaste for Bruce Dern's taciturn, petty antagonist? Or maybe I'd say it with a touch of ominous warning, like, "Hey, I bet this guy's gonna be pissed." Did I risk saying the *whole line* flat and unaffected, the way a real radioman with a hundred other tiny details he's got to be on top of and thinking about would deliver it? That would be more Method, I thought. More Meisner.

Rest assured that every movie you see where an actor delivers just one line? They've put this kind of thought into it. Sometimes you can see it. Sometimes they can hide it. But everyone who gets in front of that lens has this inner conversation. I was having mine now. I was about to speak on film.

The morning I was supposed to say my line I got a phone call. *MADtv* had been picked up. They were going to series. How much longer was I going to be on *Down Periscope*? They appreciated my work on the pilot, but they needed to nail the staff down. Should they look for someone else? We needed to start writing in a week.

Oh shit. I was slated for at least another two weeks' work on *Down Periscope*. Two weeks of pretty good pay, too—but not staff writer pay. The pay I was getting on *Down Periscope* was enough to get me into SAG and then pay a month's rent. A steady staff writing gig could pay off all of my running-across-the-collapsing-log-bridge-of-stand-up-comedy debts.

I stepped onto the submarine set for another day's filming. It was bifurcated, just the left interior, with the cameras now set to pan down from me, at the radio, to Kelsey, receiving my message and taking Admiral Graham's call.

The director called action, the camera swooped by me and I said, "There'sacallcominginforyousirAhhhhhhhhhh . . . ," and my mouth went dry.

Oh Jesus. It tumbled out in one big, moist pile of verbs. I sounded like a nineteenth-century automaton, standing in a Paris laboratory, trying to fit a four-second sentence into half a second of wax cylinder recording time. And I hadn't anticipated how hearing the word *action* and knowing that, for the first time, it actually referred to *my acting* would send all the saliva in my mouth into an adjacent dimension where people had mouths that were properly hydrated.

I coughed and cleared my throat, and David asked, Zen-like, "Would you like to do it again?" Yes, thank you, I would, please, yes.

I took a swig from the water bottle I'd hidden under the radio console as they tracked the camera back to its starting position.

"Action!"

"There's a call coming in for you, sir. Admiral Graham." Clipped, businesslike, unemotional. A submarine radioman doing his job.

"Aaaand moving on! Next setup!"

That was it. Two takes. Of course, the minute I did the second one it hit me how I might actually have done it better. I could have added even more lilt, more obliviousness to the "There's a call coming in for you, sir" line. Tee up Kelsey even better, like I'm unaware that Admiral Graham meant bad news. Would that have served the scene?

But I didn't dare ask for a third take. I'd done it in two takes, been efficient, hadn't gummed up the works. And since I was about to *seriously* gum up the works at lunchtime, I went back to my background silence. A gray-uniformed wraith.

· · · · ·

Oh man, he's going to be so pissed. I am fucked.

I was approaching David, the director, midway through lunch. He'd finished his sandwich and was chatting with the producers. My mind was racing. I was terrified.

I was about to ask to be let off of a film—a film I'd signed on to for the duration. I didn't have my agent call in and do the asking for me. That's because, at that point, I didn't have one. And I thought managers only handled club bookings and the occasional TV spot. This was the *movies*, damn it. In my mind, I had to man up and handle this myself.

"Um, David?"

David said, "Oh hey, Patton. What's up?"

"Well, there's a . . . the thing is . . ." I was stammering. Big throat-clear, and then I started again. "I wrote on a TV pilot that just got picked up. And they want me on as a staff writer. And they start next week so, uh . . . if I want the job, and I kinda need the job, y'know . . ."

David said, "It's no problem, seriously. We can fix this in just two more scenes."

"Really?" I was halfway thinking he'd blow up at me, or refer me to someone else who would say *No can do, you're fucked.*

Instead, this. A breezy "It's no problem" and a genuine, concerned and understanding smile.

"Um . . ." I was trying to think of something to say.

"We can fix it next setup. You'll see. Really, it's not a problem." Then he went back to his conversation. The whole thing was a cheery shoulder-shrug.

I went back to the hangout area near the trailers. I told everyone the next shot would be my last.

"Dude, you didn't get fired, did you?" asked Toby Huss. He and Harland were playing a complicated hand of night baseball with some of the other actors.

I said, "No, it's just I have this staff writing job, and it starts next week, and if I want to keep it, I've got to wrap things up here."

"How're you going to 'wrap things up'?" asked Harland. "We're on a submarine, aren't we?"

I hadn't thought of that. Wait, how was I going to leave a submarine?

Lunch was over and we headed back to set. I took my

seat in front of the radio console. David was talking to Kelsey. This was a major scene in the movie—Kelsey's character wins the war game with a genuinely brilliant tactical move, and we were about to shoot the obligatory "everyone cheers and celebrates" scene when we receive the news.

David looked over at me. "Patton. So, once everyone starts cheering, you get up, and clap Ken on the shoulder there, and head on down the passage toward the stern."

"I just walk away?"

David said, "Yep. Toby, take his seat at the radio for the rest of the shoot."

"Aren't people going to think it's weird?" asked Harland. "The radioman just walking away?"

"It'll puzzle the shit out of them," laughed David. "Why not?"

•••••

Down Periscope was released on March 1, 1996. My film debut. Earned my SAG card. I went to see it at the Sherman Oaks Galleria on Saturday, March 2. I saw *Harold and Maude* the night before, at the New Beverly. The next day I spent a gloomy Sunday afternoon back inside the New Beverly, getting tit-punched by *The Girl Can't Help It* and *Beyond the Valley of the Dolls*. Then I grabbed egg rolls across the street and spent a rainy evening around the corner, inside Tales Café, watching *Girls Town*. The weekend of seeing myself for the first time on the big screen was preceded by Hal Ashby's gorgeous, early seventies song fragment about love and sex in the face of annihilation and death. And then followed by the bosom-and-cartoon-obsessed celluloid limericks of Frank Tashlin, Russ Meyer* and Charles F. Haas. Ruth Gordon in *Harold and Maude*, aged and battered but clattering with hilarious life. Jayne Mansfield, Cynthia Meyers and Mamie Van Doren in *Girl*, *Beyond* and *Girls*, respectively—bulbous fuck dolls with glittering shark eyes.

And that Saturday, in a Sherman Oaks multiplex—*Down Periscope*.

Here comes my scene. Camera pans by me. I'm a gray mini-golem in my navy uniform.

"There's a call coming in for you—"

And the camera's already off of me.

"—sir. Admiral Graham." Kelsey nods and the scene proceeds with his verbally sparring with Bruce Dern on submarine radio.

A few scenes and several resolved character conflicts later Kelsey and his crew have won the war game. The bad guys have been shown up, the good guys have proved themselves and everyone's cheering. And, in the background, only visible if you're actually looking for it, is me. Heaving myself up from my radioman's chair, clapping a crewmate on the back, and then walking off, down the oval passageway and into the diesel guts of the submarine. It's not quite John Wayne at the end of

---

*And yeah, Roger Ebert—one of my no-fail guides out of the suburban gray, along with Harlan Ellison, William S. Burroughs and H. L. Mencken—squeezed *Beyond the Valley of the Dolls* from his typewriter, loins and fever dreams.

The Searchers, or Robert De Niro in the middle of *Taxi Driver*, but it's memorable all the same. In my film debut, I walk off of a submerged submarine. And I'm going to let that sentence simply end, instead of torturing a metaphor out of it.

I was happy. For better or worse, I'd made my first step to the other side of the screen. And, in the months since I'd wrapped *Down Periscope* to now, watching it with a mouthful of cineplex popcorn, I'd had an encounter that made the prospect of simply being in movies not entirely disappointing to me. I mean, I still wanted to be a director, but if that never happened . . .

Four months prior to watching myself for the first time on a movie screen I'd been, as usual, inside the New Beverly. Thursday, December 28. Three days left in 1995. Post-Christmas, empty L.A. Rain and comfortable cold. Paradise for a movie-freak moleman like myself.

I'd seen *Toy Story* earlier that day. I'd just witnessed the beginning of the Pixar revolution. Tom Hanks and Tim Allen voicing a computer-animated story about toys that also, sneakily, managed to touch on parenthood, obsolescence, and the hidden wires that run the universe and that we'll never understand. If you'd told me that twelve years and fifty pounds farther in my life I'd be the voice in a Pixar film, I'd have gently pointed out that you probably thought you were talking to Jack Black.

Now it was the evening, and I was watching *Citizen Kane* for what had to have been the tenth time (so far). The first time I'd seen it was on a tiny TV screen in a college dorm room. Now I was in a comfortably neglected, sad-spring seat near the back row of the New Beverly, watching Orson Welles's debut and, in a way, swan song unfold. *Citizen Kane* is more panoramic than most wide-screen movies, in its literal and figurative depths. I was teasing out more of its riddles, the way people will return again and again to *Ulysses* or the Rach 2.

Or *The Night Café.*

So we were fifteen minutes into the movie. *Citizen Kane* is structured in so many interdependent flashbacks that even now, having seen it close to twenty times, I couldn't tell you what was happening at that point in its story. All I know is I was rapt. The theater and world around me were gone, and I was watching Charles Foster Kane chew and bully his way to the top of a mountain he was about to go tumbling down the other side of. And he was going to drain so much love and patience and charity out of everyone he knew in the ascent that none of them would have the energy to run around the other side of that mountain to catch him when he plummeted. You know what's going to happen every single time you see it but it's such a sweet ride—like bodysurfing a wave that you know is going to send you belly-first into abrasive sand; still, you can never resist the swell when you feel it rise.

But there was noise behind me—a rumbling, human-but-maybe-not-human gurgle and bark. Someone was sitting down, fifteen minutes into *Citizen Kane*, and they were talking to no one. Out loud. *Goddamn it.* I turned around to shush whoever was pulling me out of Welles's cinematic gravity.*

It was Lawrence Tierney. *Reservoir Dogs* Lawrence Tierney. Bar-brawling, knife-wound-surviving, battling bruiser T-shirted human tank Lawrence Tierney. Sitting alone in the dark behind me, watching *Citizen Kane*.

I didn't shush him.

For about fifteen minutes he sat there, talking to the screen as if he were just out of view to the other characters, admonishing Kane. "Don't clap for that squawking bitch, she can't sing. Siddown, ya chump!" "Aw Jesus, what's he staring at? You gonna cry, fancy man?" It was the best DVD commentary I've ever heard.

Suddenly there was a younger man behind him. His handler, I found out later from Sherman. A young kid who'd landed the exhausting, unenviable job of attempt-

---

*The New Beverly—like all rep theaters—had its usual cast of jabbering weirdos. It also had the occasional clueless Very Successful Interloper who'd end up being even more infuriating than the half-broken sprocket fiends who'd mutter along with Warren Beatty in *McCabe and Mrs. Miller* or sing along with Eugene Pallette as he descended the stairs near the end of *The Lady Eve*. One particularly smug, self-satisfied, midnineties sitcom megastar decided to grace a screening of Albert Brooks's near-perfect *Modern Romance*, and proceeded to talk over the movie, full volume, adding brilliant shadings and observations like "Nice jacket" and "His record collection sucks." When I finally leaned forward and asked him to Shut. The. Fuck. Up, he looked back at me with open pity and a sad shake of his head, as if to say, "This poor bastard doesn't even know how lucky he is to hear me talking over this movie." I'm proud to say I've never watched a single episode of his zeitgeist-grabbing ensemble show and I'll say proudly, on my deathbed, "I made it all the way through the flesh carnival without seeing a second of that thing. But I've seen *Modern Romance* ten times, three of them probably to spite him and his friends." Glorious.

ing to guide a driverless tractor of a human being like Lawrence Tierney through his remaining days.

"Larry! How long you been in here? We gotta go!"

Lawrence said, "We do? Yeah?"

"Yeah. They're waiting."

Lawrence stood up. He considered the screen one last time.

"I ain't never seen this cocksucker," he said. " 'S not half bad."

And then he was gone.

This was a professional actor, a noir icon who'd end up with a more-than-fifty-year career. And he'd never seen *Citizen Kane*. But the fifteen out-of-context minutes he's just watched—after missing the first fifteen—weren't "half bad."

I'd just started working in movies. One vaporous bit part. I'd tried to make it count. But I forgot something.

It's the doing it, over and over again, exactly like stand-up comedy. You did it until your mouth didn't dry up in front of a camera and you forgot the lens was there and you kept on doing it. The career and the bigger roles (and maybe the directing?) would happen without your thinking about it. No matter how deeply a movie pulled you into its orbit, there was always someone else— whether they were a screen lifer like Lawrence Tierney or a happy businessman with no desire to live on celluloid— who would merely be happy for the momentary distraction. That was the best I could hope for, at the beginning. The swooping and gliding and changing people's lives, like I'd grandiosely imagined when I watched *Sunset Bou-*

levard and *Ace in the Hole*? That would be partially up to me, partially up to the audience, and partially up to time itself. Lawrence Tierney giving *Citizen Kane* a "not half bad" in the New Beverly on a rainy December night was something I took with me when I watched *Down Periscope* three months later.

Not half bad. A start.

CHAPTER FIVE

Meat and Potatoes

Los Angeles,
August 1995

By August of 1995 I was firmly inserted into an office chair at Ren-Mar Studios (formerly Desilu, home of both *I Love Lucy* and *Star Trek*), writing sketches for *MADtv*. I was also beginning to expand myself, physically, from relying on craft service snacks and endless sessions playing *Doom* and *Quake* to relieve the tension and boredom of writer's block. The days of pacing back and forth on comedy club stages plus working out in hotel gyms on the road were over. The lean was turning into small shelves of flab, which would solidify into the bureau of drawers I currently have perched on my chest and abdomen. Maybe I needed to learn that I only needed the "sock drawer" equivalent of food to get through a day.

Eventually.

But back then, still in my carb-burning twenties, I didn't see the flesh avalanche coming. I didn't see a lot of things happening around me. Like my bosses' growing frustration with my constant whining about our show's not being more innovative. Or my then-girlfriend's disillusion with our relationship. Or a lot of my friends' avoidance of me, especially if there was the threat of movies entering the conversation. I had been an Asperger's-y movie fan when I got to Los Angeles three months earlier. And now? After scoping out where all of the first-run, rep, museum and campus screenings were? I was a jabbering, repellent acolyte.

Oh man. I just looked at my old calendar pages from May of 1995 through July of the same year? And keep in mind—I was writing down *every* movie I saw in a movie theater. And *only* theater viewings. So this wasn't counting movies I watched on TV—either broadcast or on VHS or a then-rare DVD.

Just in theaters: twenty-two films. Some old classics like *Kiss of Death* and *Steamboat Bill, Jr.* New, quality films like *Muriel's Wedding* and *Crumb*. But mostly crap.

Crap either because it'd come out and I wanted to see everything (*Die Hard with a Vengeance*, *Batman Forever*) or crap because it was in one of my Five Movie Books.

Bloodsucking Freaks (Sunday, June 18, at the Sunset 5 at midnight), for instance, which had some weirdly brilliant performances because the director, Joel M. Reed, pulled his cast from experienced off-Broadway actors. It's a schizophrenic experience, watching that movie. Cheap gore and clumsy gallows humor delivered with genuine panache and skill. The disconnect is more disturbing than the red Karo syrup dripping off of the obvious mannequin body parts. Or *Maniac*, on another Sunday at midnight at the Sunset 5.* Now that I think of it, they were doing some sort of exploitation film festival on successive Sundays. I was determined to see every single one. They were all listed in *The Psychotronic Encyclopedia of Film*, anyway. Who cared that I was showing up for Monday morning pitch meetings sleep deprived, incoherent and still coughing up shards of popcorn kernel husks? I was becoming a *director*.

And now we get to August of 1995. The mustard

---

*The director of *Maniac*, Bill Lustig, was there to introduce that screening. A Latino couple, dressed in black leather, sat beside me holding their sleeping baby. It never once woke up, during all of the screaming and stabbings and shotgun blasts of *Maniac*. Bill introduced his masterpiece succinctly: "I made this film on a wing and a prayer back in 1979. It stars Joe Spinell—" At that moment the Latino dad barked out, "Joe Spinell fuckin' *rules*!" Bill answered, "God bless you. Joe's dead now. Okay, so I'll be in the lobby after if any of you have questions. On second thought, no. I won't. I won't be there. Enjoy the film."

sunshine daggers of late-summer Los Angeles throbbed through the slats of my office window. And once it got dark, and relatively cool, I'd be off to the movies.

This is what one month's movie menu looked like:

Friday, August 4,

Dr. Strangelove, or How I Learned to Stop Worrying and Love the Bomb **at the New Beverly**

I skipped a Friday night *MADtv* taping to go see this, which was probably my third viewing at that point. But it was the first of mine on the big screen and, seeing as it was listed in two of my Five Movie Books, a can't-miss.

I've seen this movie at least four more times since that screening, but this is the one I remember the most. Probably because I was so thirsty to receive it. I'd spent the day struggling with some half-assed sketch idea of mine that I couldn't find an engine for, a nebulous half-a-joke that stared back at me from my Mac's screen like a snide drunk I was facing down in a bar. And now—Kubrick. Especially in *Strangelove*, a movie at once sprawling and precise, inhuman and tragic.

I remember this screening because, when Peter Sellers appears for the first time as Strangelove, reversing himself in his wheelchair (while keeping his head at the same jaunty angle and his smile in the same forced rictus as FDR), the crowd I was seeing it with exploded with applause. And we'd already seen him as Colonel Mandrake and President Muffley. But here he was, a much-imitated, recontextualized pop culture reference, springing up from his place of origin. Imitation leads to exhilaration when you follow it back to its source.

I left the screening feeling recharged in my nascent comedy snobbery. If Kubrick could wring laughs from nuclear annihilation at the height of the Cold War, while also throwing in Nazis, sexual frustration and the beginning of the nerds vs. jocks schism (Sellers's Muffley vs. George C. Scott's General Turgidson), then I should be going even farther with my sketches, with my stand-up, right?

Sunday, August 6,
La Jetée at the New Beverly

Chris Marker's moody, near-motionless meditation on the costs of time travel and nostalgia—barely half an hour long but leaving you feeling like you'd just been dragged through a lifetime's worth of emotion and loss. This must have been showing with other movies—*Sans Soleil*? Maybe a Tarkovsky? But all I wrote down was *La Jetée*.

To go from Kubrick's massive, orchestral doomsday screwball to, two days later, Marker's elegant single postapocalypse stanza was the kind of thrilling drop that only the true film freak gets to experience. It's like driving, listening to the radio, being completely at the whim of whatever the deejay wants to play. Instead of some perfect mix tape that you've assembled, making you thus fully aware of the shifts in tone to come, you surf in the foam of chance. I drove cross-country in 1992 and one night outside of Denver, listening to a classic rock station, the end of Pink Floyd's "Breathe (Reprise)" was winding down. The words "to hear the softly spoken magic spells" floated away on the highway ink. And then a beat of silence and then Elton John's "Saturday Night's Alright for Fighting" sneered out of the speakers, a hilarious, drunken youthful rebuke to Roger Waters's morose musings on wasted time. I remember laughing out loud at the gear-stripping brilliance of the reversal.

I felt the same way leaving that Sunday afternoon screening of *La Jetée*. Only I wasn't laughing. Again, I was frustrated, seeing two more of the extremes that film could exist at. I was writing on a sketch show for the Fox network. Why wasn't I summoning and executing brilliance like that in the stuff I pitched? Why was I being so lazy?

Wednesday, August 9, *The Bicycle Thief* at the New Beverly

The first and only time I've ever seen this. I probably need to see it again, now that I'm a dad. At the time, in my twenties and thinking I'd never get married or burden myself with kids (I needed all the sleep I could get if I was going to make all of the before-dawn call times a director has to deal with), I loved this film academically. Recovering a stolen bicycle becomes as edge-of-your-seat important as, say, blowing up a Death Star or defeating a twenty-five-foot killer shark. A quick meal of fried bread is the equivalent to the father and son bonding over the table, of a warrior's victory banquet. You're rooting for two people you probably see a dozen times a day, in a 7-Eleven, in line at the DMV. It's the kind of movie that makes you realize that each person you glance at, interact with or ignore is an epic film or thrilling novel you'll never get to experience. Makes you bless the grandeur of life and curse it at the same time for being too painfully narrow and brief.

What if I could successfully pitch a sketch about a guy just trying to retrieve a wallet he left at a Laundromat? Could I smuggle even a small slice of *The Bicycle Thief* into a filmed short for *MADtv*? Would they let me direct it?

Thursday, August 17, *Hiroshima Mon Amour* at the New Beverly

I know people hold this and *The Seventh Seal* up as examples of why art films or foreign films suck, but for once? The dullards are right. I hated this movie when I saw it in college but I had to see it again to make sure. It wasn't even in one of my Five Movie Books. But I watched it and it pissed me off all over again and ended up confusing me, a year later, when I went to see Resnais's *Last Year at Marienbad*, which is an even bigger arty-farty *fuck you* and I ended up really liking it.

Sigh.

Saturday, August 19,
Belle de Jour at the Los Feliz 3

Buñuel made this movie in 1967, fer chrissakes. That's all I kept thinking when I was watching it. Casual prostitution, and boredom, and boredom with sex treated hilariously? And what was in that *box*? None of the whores would agree to its owner's entreaty, before Catherine Deneuve shrugged her flawless shoulders and all but looked at the camera like a Flintstones animal appliance muttering, "It's a living."

Something shocking, something that goes too far—that's where my thinking has to be from now on, I raged to myself, leaving the theater and crossing Vermont Street to the House of Pies for a late evening slice of pecan and some coffee. *It's 1995, fer chrissakes. Kurt Cobain and GG Allin are dead. What the hell am I doing with my life?*

Friday, August 25,
Kids at the Sunset 5

Here it was. Here was the next shocking thing, as far as I was concerned. I was mesmerized by the energy and heat and sweat and cum up on the screen. It made me resee my teenage, suburban years as maybe not so bland as I remember them. Because I suddenly remembered the constant, tormenting fuck-throb of adolescence, how it yanked and shoved me in some pretty embarrassing directions, how I could scorch away the wick of an entire day on the distant promise of sex or even a glimpse of female flesh. There I was, up on the screen, fractured into a dozen different inarticulate, real characters, pinging around a grimy New York City on an even hotter summer day than the one in *Do the Right Thing*. That movie ended with a racial apocalypse. *Kids* begins and ends with a sexual one, only it's an apocalypse at plague pace. I've never seen *Kids* again. I haven't needed to.

I ought to point a camera at my life. Or the people around me, I thought, leaving that screening. I had that weekend before a Monday morning *MADtv* pitch meeting. Now I had Buñuel, and a stolen bicycle and Slim Pickens riding a nuclear warhead and teenage lust and the heartbreak of time travel in my head. I think I went out the next night and got Russian-wedding drunk at the sketchiest bar I could find. I probably ended up staring at the sky while the scotch and ginger ale detached my mind from my body. I was going to pull down the universe and strain its essence through a comedy sketch, is what I probably thought. Scotch-drunk. Film-drunk. Self-drunk.

Monday, August 28, eleven a.m.
MADtv pitch meeting

My head feels like a rotted cantaloupe, and my body is a single corpse in a cosmic, mass grave. I've got three pages of handwritten notes—partially from Saturday night (illegible) and partially from that Monday morning (trying to decipher the drunken, roller-coaster penmanship over McDonald's coffee and a McMuffin).

Garry Campbell and Brian Hartt, both veterans of *The Kids in the Hall*, have each finished their individual pitches. Brilliant, as always. Brian is weeks away from becoming the head writer. Then Blaine Capatch, my office-mate, pitches six or seven wicked, literate, oddball sketches.

Over to me.

"What if . . . now, follow me here . . ."

Everyone's following me. Go ahead.

"It's a bunch of kids . . . like, younger. In their early twenties. And there's been this apocalypse. They're living in ruins. The ruins of Los Angeles. You can just make out it's Los Angeles in the ruins. And there's this one girl we're following, her mom, you see, is working in this brothel. Like, okay, wait. They've turned a ruined bicycle shop into a brothel. And there are these mutants coming in who want to do certain sex acts.

"Okay, no, wait. What the sketch is about is, there's this brothel in this postnuclear wasteland, and it's a younger girl in her twenties, and she's arguing with her mom about how uncool her mom is about not being up on all of the new mutant sex acts that everyone's doing.

"But what we reveal, what we do as a twist is show that the mom is actually a time traveler, and it's the mom taking her daughter, uh, forward in time, because she's worried that her daughter getting into skateboarding will lead her to drugs or dangerous sex, only the mom is such a hysterical prude that she's zapped them forward to this crazy, violent, postapocalyptic scenario. It's like the mom is saying, 'See where all the skateboarding is going to take you?' Only this is the mom's overkill method of doing that.

"And then what's worse for the mom is that her daughter still isn't shocked, and is more embarrassed that her mom is too uptight to have weird, uh, tentacle sex with mutants.

"Oh, and we could do it in segments, and keep interspersing it throughout the episode, little short films that, when you get to the end, tell this whole story. It'd be really, uh, innovative."

Silence. Then Adam Small, one of the executive producers, with the poise and patience of a saint, says, "Well, write up a version. Let's see it on paper."

"Yeah, okay. I'll give you a better idea what I'm talking about."

Then I go back to my office, play *Doom* for two hours, and write a sketch about a really dumb doughnut shop employee. They don't use it. They're right.

This is the first time it hits me—maybe I need to change my life.

Two days later, Wednesday, August 30, I'm back at the New Beverly, seeing a double feature of *Blow Out* and *Dressed to Kill*.

"You really only need to see *Blow Out*," says Sherman, tearing my ticket. "*Dressed to Kill*'s kind of a mess."

But they're both in *The Psychotronic Encyclopedia*, so I'm in for the duration. And, as it turns out when *Dressed to Kill* ends? Sherman was right. I really only needed to see *Blow Out*.

Less movies, more living. That's what I'm saying to myself as I walk out onto the street. Gonna make that change, soon . . .

But a few more hits of celluloid can't hurt, right?

Or maybe a massive, brain-shorting overdose?

CHAPTER SIX

Overdosing

Los Angeles,
October 21–22, 1995

13	14	15
286/79	287/78	288/77
THE ABOMINABLE SNOWMAN OF THE HIMALAYAS	HOUND OF THE BASKERVILLES HORROR OF DRACULA	NEVER TAKE SWEETS FROM A STRANGER
STOLEN FACE	THE STRANGLERS OF BOMBAY	SCREAM OF FEAR
CURSE OF FRANKEN-STEIN	THESE ARE THE DAMNED	DGA ✔
DGA ✔	MADTV PREMIER ✔ DGA ✔	
20	21	22
293/72	294/71	295/70
	Revenge of FRANKENSTEIN	X THE UNKNOWN WHEN DINOSAURS RULED THE EARTH
"BOOZE BAGS" at Theatre Theater ✔	Die! Die! MY DARLING THE MUMMY PREHISTORIC WOMEN THE VAMPIRE LOVERS THE Reptile PLAGUE OF THE ZOMBIES CHAPLIN THEATER ✔	5 MILLION MILES to EARTH FRANKENSTEIN MUST BE DESTROYED CAPTAIN KRONOS: VAMPIRE HUNTER CHAPLIN THEATER ✔
27	28	29
300/65	301/64	302/63 Daylight Savings Time Ends
FRANKENStein & DRACULA @ the ORPHEUM ✔	Leaving Las Vegas Beverly cinemas, HIGH SIERRA New BEVERLY ✔	Get SHORTY Galaxy Cinema ✔

A shimmering, satanic, alien insect head is hovering over London and I can't remember if the dinosaurs are coming back or not.

I've spent all of an autumn weekend, Saturday and Sunday, both days starting at ten a.m. inside the DGA Theater, watching a marathon Hammer film festival.

With a few exceptions, it's a very rich, color-saturated marathon. It's a marathon where I'm seeing a lot of the same people over and over again. Peter Cushing. Christopher Lee. The indispensable, sad-eyed Michael Ripper. Buxom women with creamy skin and tight, frightened mouths and impeccable diction.

The first day whips by in quick succession: *The Revenge of Frankenstein*, *Die! Die! My Darling!*, *The Mummy*, *Prehistoric Women*, *The Vampire Lovers*, *The Reptile*, *The Plague of the Zombies*. When Tallulah Bankhead had her meltdown near the end of *Die! Die! My Darling!* and broke out her secret stash of forbidden lipstick, I was still four hours away from Ingrid Pitt's bathtub scene in *The Vampire Lovers* (and the fang marks on many a heaving bosom). It was midnight when I staggered out onto the darkened lot, the plot and details of *The Plague of the Zombies* already leaking out of my skull forever. I got home, checked off my *Psychotronic Encyclopedia* and went to sleep.

Only to wake up the next morning at eight, eat a hurried breakfast and head back to DGA for a ten a.m. screening of *X: The Unknown*. Followed by *When Dinosaurs Ruled the Earth*, *Five Million Years to Earth* (*Cult Movies* volume 3!!!), *Frankenstein Must Be Destroyed* and *Captain Kronos: Vampire Hunter*.

Playwright Jack Gelber, who penned *The Connection*, wrote an interesting essay about overdosing on films. He was living in New York in the sixties, when Times Square was a bleak, sleazy wasteland and the all-day, all-night grindhouse theaters ruled the landscape. And, in the middle of a personal crisis, he spent several sleepless days wandering from one theater to the next, watching film after film, nonstop. And he got to a point where all of the films he had seen—gangster pictures, Westerns, schlocky sex romps and Z-grade horror movies—started to blend together into one massive, daymare-fueled meganarrative. Humphrey Bogart and Randolph Scott having sex with space aliens.

Now, on a Sunday evening, near the end of the brilliant *Five Million Years to Earth*, when our scientist hero, Quatermass, is realizing that maybe our perceptions of God and the devil are just psychic mind-slog from a crashed alien spaceship, and the Very Very British James Donald is riding the construction crane into the glowing insect alien's head to destroy the vision virus that's infecting the planet, I experienced . . . slippage.

I was partially exhausted, which didn't help. But suddenly the alien insect head turned into Tallulah Bankhead's face, hovering over Hobbs End, London, screaming about lipstick and God. Mummies, cavewomen and lesbian vampires came spilling out of her mouth. A gigantic Peter Cushing, tight-lipped and driven as Dr. Frankenstein, appeared to sew Tallulah's mouth shut. But her hellish progeny were loose on the streets, and somewhere nearby Christopher Lee opened the door to the reptile woman's cage and she pounced on the shambling mummy, sinking her tusky fangs into his powdery, rotted shoulder.

I blinked, hard. I was awake. I'd made friends with a schoolteacher named Dana, who was also there for the duration. He seemed more amused by the lineup of films than I was. He also, probably, didn't have a pagan shrine of Five Movie Books crouching at home for him to check the titles off in. He wasn't quite the sprocket fiend, like me, with absolutely nothing else to do on a weekend but stack it with films. Oh shit, I realize now I was judging him.

Dana had one arm. He'd lost the other one to cancer. Being the film freak I was, I never bothered to ask about it further. Or even what his last name was. Not enough time before or between the films. A one-armed schoolteacher, teaching kids in the shitty L.A. school district, probably full of more stories and personality than the electric fables being projected above us. But I was more focused on the mummies and vampires and dinosaurs and aliens to take a deeper interest in an actual, unique human being sitting right next to me. Such was my addiction, at that point. Cut off from the world. A ghost, but breathing and jacketed with flesh.

I looked over at Dana and he must have seen something in my eyes.

"You okay?" he whispered.

I said, "All of these . . . these movies are kind of blending . . ."

Dana laughed and then suppressed it. "I know what you mean. It's kind of cool, isn't it?"

I didn't say anything. I was dead set on a course of cutting off more and more human contact in my life—of cutting off more and more life—so that I could devour more movies. You know, to become a director. Though, I imagine, you should probably know something about human dimensions, and connections, and all the facets of emotion, if you're ever going to want to put anything memorable on-screen. Like *Casablanca*.

Or *Kids*.

But all I was focused on, in the initial heat of my addiction, were the two dimensions of the screen and the ritual of the Five Books.

Five Million Years to Earth ended and *Frankenstein Must Be Destroyed* began. It was eight p.m. on a Sunday night. Peter Cushing is extraordinary in that movie, and even my exhaustion fog and slippage couldn't dilute Cushing's sharp-edged, misanthropic tour-de-force in what is hands-down Hammer Films' best Frankenstein movie.

Halfway through the movie, after Dr. Frankenstein has charmed and sweet-talked the widow of a man he's secretly cut up and restitched into what will be a confused, pathetic monster, Cushing turns to the camera—to his two unwilling associates—and barks, "*PACK*. We're leaving!"

It's a verbal gunshot, and it's the last thing I remember from this two-day Iditarod of cinema. *Captain Kronos: Vampire Hunter* started immediately after *Frankenstein Must Be Destroyed* ended. Caroline Munro is in that one. I can't remember a single frame. I sat there. I stared at the screen while it was projected. I couldn't tell you a single thing about it.

Dana and I walked out of the empty DGA Theater. Midnight. Twelve movies in two days.

"We made it," said Dana, grinning.

"We did," I said. We stood there.

"Well, I'll see you," said Dana. I think my glazed, jittery-pupiled look unnerved him. He walked away, west down Sunset, three blocks east of where I'd parked. I watched him go and then, eerily enough, stopped myself from saying, "*PACK*. We're leaving!" out loud.

I wasn't leaving any time soon. Not the world of the sprocket fiend, that's for sure. I found out, one year later, that the addiction could follow me anywhere. Even back home to Virginia.

CHAPTER SEVEN

You Can, Unfortunately, Go Home Again

Sterling, Virginia,
Thanksgiving 1996

11 VETERANS DAY REMEMBRANCE DAY (CANADA)	12	13	14 THE NEXT BIG THING Hackney Gold Screening Room ✓
18	19	20	21 IMPROV ✓
25 •	26 LARGER THAN LIFE Tournament 3 ✓ ViRG	27 LAST MAN STANDING Herndon Twin ✓ STAR TREK: FIRST CONTACT Reston Tournament ✓ iNiD	28 THANKSGIVING DAY

I'm sitting in a movie theater in Northern Virginia, hating my best friend from childhood.

It's Wednesday, November 27. I'm home visiting my family for Thanksgiving. I've got days to kill afterward, except I have to kill them back in my hometown, which is difficult.

First, most of my friends have moved away. Either completely out of state, to new lives and families and jobs, or to suburbs or towns so far away that navigating the DC metro traffic just to see them would, coming and going, eat up an entire day for what would probably amount to an hour or so of awkward conversation. At least it seems awkward to me. What's wrong with people? All they want to yak about is their kids or places they've traveled to or divorces or affairs or encounters they've had in bars or at weddings or family reunions. Don't they want to talk about the movies of the newly rediscovered French crime master Jean-Pierre Melville, or the Dogme 95 movement, or the dozen or so hidden references in the latest Tarantino film? Why are people so *boring*?

And then I got a call. The first friend I made in Virginia, when my family moved there from Tustin Meadows when I was five. My dad decided to make Northern Virginia our permanent home after that move. Good-bye, blond hair and suntan. Hello, pasty pudginess.*

"I'm here visiting my folks," he said. "You free one of these days? I'm here 'til Saturday."

I said, "So am I! Yeah, what do you want to do?"

"I dunno. I may be busy nights, actually, with all these relatives coming in."

I said, "Then let's go to Hunan Gardens in Herndon some afternoon, then go catch a movie next door."

He laughed. Hunan Gardens was a strip mall Chinese/ Polynesian restaurant that, when we were seventeen,

---

*Sure, I'll rewrite the facts to make it seem like it was the *state of Virginia* that forced me to be inert, be addicted to carbs and shun the sun. Allow an old man some delusional comfort, won't you?

would serve us those big-ass tiki-style alcoholic drinks without bothering to look at our IDs. Going back there now, on a Wednesday afternoon, sipping Zombies and Scorpions out of skull-and volcano-shaped ceramic mugs, was boozy nostalgia at its best.

Next door to Hunan Gardens was a second-run movie theater. The Herndon Twin. Movies for $2. Gone now, of course. But in 1996? It was my old suburb's closest approximation to the New Beverly.

Not that they were showing Ozus or Chabrols to the housewives and night-shift workers of Herndon. In our case, full of rum and fried rice and swaying in the bracing November afternoon air, we could choose between Bill Murray in *Larger Than Life* or Bruce Willis in *Last Man Standing*.

"Willis," said my friend. I agreed. Two tickets. Just like at the New Beverly, our ticket seller tore our stubs. I wondered if he resold the other half of the tickets, like I used to when I worked at the Towncenter 3, pocketing the money to spend on cassette tapes later. I wouldn't have blamed the poor guy. We were the only ones in the theater.

So my friend and I chatted for a while. Gossip about mutual friends from childhood—who's married, or divorced, or living back home with the folks. I told him stories about Los Angeles, about some of the more colorful, difficult guest stars on *MADtv*. He told me about his job, about how they were trying to "put the company on a page on the Internet" so people could "shop at [the company] with their computers." Neither of us could see, in the long run, how that would work.

We were a couple of minutes from the movie starting and I chuckled. To him, it seemed as if I was laughing at nothing specific.

"What's funny?"

I said, "Not really *funny*. But what's weird about this movie is, it's a remake of an Italian film, which was itself a remake of a Japanese film, which itself was based on an American crime novel."

My friend stared at me.

"This movie is *Fistful of Dollars*, basically. Which was an Italian film. And that was a remake of *Yojimbo*, you know, the Kurosawa film, with Toshiro Mifune? And Kurosawa based *Yojimbo* on Dashiell Hammett's *Red Harvest*. And this movie is based on *Red Harvest*, but it got there by way of *Fistful of Dollars* and *Yojimbo*."

My friend continued to stare at me.

"Never say Hollywood doesn't have new ideas," I said. And gave him a laugh.

He stared at me another moment and then leaned in, close. "Why . . . did . . . you . . . *bring* me to this thing?"

He seemed deeply angry. I couldn't figure out where the anger was coming from. The lights went down and *Last Man Standing* began.

It's not a good film. I love Walter Hill, and the cast is nothing but reassuring favorites—Willis, and Christopher Walken, and hey, there's Bruce Dern and William Sanderson and David Patrick Kelly, he of the clinking, bottles-on-fingers Luther from *The Warriors*. But sometimes a lot of terrific people come together with stellar source material and even the right idea about filming it (dusty,

Prohibition-era starkness) but, to paraphrase John Huston, "the thing doesn't happen."

It doesn't happen in *Last Man Standing*.

Not that I have time to think about it. My friend takes full advantage of the fact that we're alone in the theater together to emit a steady stream of heavy "Uuuccccccchhhhh" sighs and "Who the hell is this guy?" and "I can't even follow this" complaints. "Is this supposed to be a samurai thing?" he asks at one point, when all the characters are eating a spaghetti dinner.

The movie reaches its dusty, wheezy, bloody conclusion and we walk out into the early evening.

"Well that made zero sense. Seriously, why'd you take me to that thing?" my friend complains.

I'm speechless for a moment. I gather my thoughts and say, gently, "It was . . . come on, it was so simple. He's in town, there's two gangs fighting, he plays them against each—"

My friend cuts me off. "Italian movie based on a Japanese movie based on some old book? Why'd you tell me that?"

I say, "What's that got to do with anything? None of that was in the movie. It's a straightforward—"

"Why'd you put that in my head?"

I'm dumbfounded. I can't conceive that knowing all of the details about the making of a film—especially one with a hilariously convoluted route to conception like *Last Man Standing*—can be anything but pleasurable.

But it isn't. Not to him. And, in the next moment, I realize what it is.

Movies, to him and the majority of the planet, are an enhancement to a life. The way a glass of wine complements a dinner. I'm the other way around. I'm the kind of person who eats a few bites of food so that my stomach can handle the full bottle of wine I'm about to drink.

No, wait. I'm lying. I'm realizing that *now*. Back then, in the lobby of the Herndon Twin, I'm pitying my friend and disgusted at his narrow-minded, suburban view of films. In my world, seeing an afternoon matinee of *Last Man Standing* should be a prelude to driving into DC, maybe catching *Rashomon* or *The Earrings of Madame de . . .* at a rep theater. This idiot wants to go to a bar, maybe watch a sporting event and talk to people, play cards, socialize.

What a waste, I think, slipping deeper into my addiction.

I get back to Los Angeles that Sunday. That evening I'm at the ticket booth of the New Beverly, buying a ticket to see Jackie Chan's *Drunken Master*.

"I didn't see you this week," says Sherman, handing me my stub.

"I went back home for Thanksgiving."

He asks, "See any movies?"

I mutter, "*Yojimbo*." Then I go inside, and eat the fried rice I bought from across the street, and watch Jackie Chan drunkenly kick and punch his way through an army of bad guys. Internally, I kick and punch myself deeper into my addiction.

But I'll be directing soon. Only not in the way I always imagined it.

CHAPTER EIGHT

The Day the Clown Didn't Cry

The Powerhouse Theatre,
January 27, 1997

12	13	14
BREAKING THE WAVES Los Feliz 3 ✓ NIGHT OF THE HUNTER Tales Café ✓		
19	20 MARTIN LUTHER KING, JR. DAY	21
"HAMLET ['96] Royal ✓		
26	27	28
BETRAYED Tales Café ✓	"The DAY The CLOWN CRIED" POWERHOUSE THEATER ✓	

"Chevy Chase was *born* to play a clown who leads children into a gas oven!"

That's Bob Odenkirk, onstage at the Powerhouse Theatre in Santa Monica, improvising one of the most brilliant lines in a brilliant night of comedy that me and all of my friends had to lash together at the last minute. I'd been handed a cease-and-desist order one hour before the show started. Jerry Lewis was pissed and threatening legal action. Or, at least, that's what I initially thought. It turned out to be even worse, and, tragically, funnier than that. You'll see. Let me give you a little background here.

It was my twenty-eighth birthday. The year before, I'd gotten my hands on the shooting script of Jerry Lewis's *The Day the Clown Cried*. It was a drama about a clown in Auschwitz, forced by the Nazis to entertain Jewish children on their way to the gas chamber. If he does this, his life will be spared. But his conscience can't bear the burden, so, at the last minute, he enters the gas chamber with them. Slam. Hiss. Fade to black.

The script was originally written by Joan O'Brien and Charles Denton. But when Jerry Lewis decided to make it, he made . . . revisions. Slapstick. Pratfalls. A scene where it's so cold in the concentration camp barracks that the clown—named Helmut Doork—pisses ice. I wish I was making this up. No, wait, no I don't.

It was glorious. As Harry Shearer wrote, in a *Spy* magazine article about actually being able to see the movie, "It was like going down to Tijuana and seeing a painting on black velvet of Auschwitz."

The tortured history of *The Day the Clown Cried* has been recounted elsewhere. The legends that have grown around it are contradictory, fascinating and exhausting.

My deal was simple: I'd gotten my hands on a copy of the script. I pared it down to a manageable length, saving all of the most Jerry Lewis–ian scenes, and started doing live readings of it at the Largo.

I gathered together all of my comedian friends and assigned them multiple roles. All except for the role of the clown, which only ever went to one actor, since that person had to do all of the heavy lifting. Toby Huss performed it first, brilliantly. He'd do the clown part as a frightened, fey German when he was interacting with other adults. But for the scenes where he entertained the kids, he'd suddenly be a mean, short-fused, no-patience Frank Sinatra. Later on, due to Toby's increasingly crazy work schedule in TV and film, Jay Johnston (from *Mr. Show*) inherited the role, doing a one-man tour-de-force of distilled Jerry Lewis mawkishness and spastic clowning, oftentimes in the same moment.

And I was directing! Well, kind of. I mean, I had to figure out who to cast where, and make sure everyone was in the right position when they'd step forward, and . . . oh, fuck it, this was the farthest from "directing" anything you can be, but it was something. Plus, my friends were all better, more experienced stage actors than me, so I wasn't so much directing as staying out of their way.

I never advertised the show, at first. It was invite-only.

But word got around. Jerry Lewis's take on the Holocaust is a unique creature of discomfort and a dirty jewel to behold. And after three hush-hush performances at the Largo, I got a call from *LA Weekly*. They wanted to make the next reading their "Pick of the Week."

This next bit is my fault. I should've politely said no and kept it quiet, but my ambition and hunger for fame got the better of me, and I said sure. So they called, and I did a brief interview, and the next week there it was, in a box alongside their other pick of the week, *Full House*'s Dave Coulier in concert somewhere. "Patton Oswalt Presents A Staged Reading of Jerry Lewis' *The Day the Clown Cried*" at the Powerhouse Theatre in Santa Monica. In the paragraph I said a few pithy, oh-so-ironic things about how inane a script it was, that the idea of Jerry Lewis playing a clown at Auschwitz who's forced to entertain children on their way to the gas ovens was, from that description alone, something that would spill out of the mouth of Joyce Carol Oates or Richard Brautigan, rather than the star of *Cinderfella* and *The Nutty Professor*.

Fast-forward to the day of the show. I was at the Powerhouse early, waiting for the cast to arrive. Every single seat had been grabbed the moment we announced the reading. Again, not charging admission. Simply offering the spectacle.

I walked up to the theater and there was a man standing on the sidewalk. Try to imagine an even skinnier, even seedier-looking John Waters. A "suit" that was a sport coat desperately matched with an almost-the-same-color pair of slacks. He was holding a sheet of paper. I approached him. He threw it at me. It had no weight, so it fluttered in concentric arcs until one end of the paper hit my pant leg.

"You've been served, Mr. Osweld." And then he stalked away.

I picked up the paper. It was a cease-and-desist order on the reading. Do not proceed with the performance or face legal action. I glanced over it a few more times and headed inside the theater.

"What's up?" asked the manager.

I said, "I think Jerry Lewis just hit us with a cease-and-desist order. He found out about the reading and is shutting us down." I'll admit I felt a little shaky. What sort of power did Jerry Lewis still hold in Hollywood?

"That's awesome!" said the manager.

I wasn't so sure. The Powerhouse Theatre had been named in the letter, and I didn't want them getting dragged into any trouble. The theater's phone started ringing. It was the law firm that had just presented me with the letter. After a few terse phone conversations, the theater manager didn't find the situation so awesome. The cast—and the audience—was starting to arrive. What the fuck were we supposed to do?

I sat the cast down—a group that included not only Toby Huss but also David Cross, Bob Odenkirk, Paul F. Tompkins, Brian Posehn, Laura Milligan, Scott Aukerman and Dave Foley from *The Kids in the Hall*. I told them the predicament I was in. I suggested we go out and just improvise, on the fly, a show about being canceled, about being shut down.

Most of my friends were cool about it. They were game to try. Cross, as usual, was defiant.

He said, "Let me see the letter."

I handed it to him. The theater manager came backstage and said someone was there to talk to me. He looked a little shaken.

I walked out to the empty lawn in the back of the theater and was confronted by the single douchiest-looking adult male I'd ever seen. All of the worst aspects of 1) a jock, 2) a shrill NPR listener, 3) a wannabe alpha male and 4) a movie producer, which, it turned out, he was. Or, at least, he said he was.

He said, "I just hosted a party at the Sundance Film Festival for *six hundred people*." That was his way of introducing himself. This was before he said his name, come to think of it.

"Um, that's, uh—"

"And now I gotta come home to my five-room house in Malibu, and I find out a bunch of C-list actors are reading a script that I've optioned?" said the Kale Salad Eater with Rage Issues.

"Well, we're not charging any money for it, and it's—"

The Hot Yoga Enthusiast's face turned purple with wrath and he spat, "Oh *fuck you*, that doesn't matter! It doesn't matter and you *know* it fucking doesn't goddamned cocksucking matter!!!" I felt sorry for his desktop Zen sand garden when he got home later that night. His yin-yang peace-symbol necklace charm bobbed up and down on his chest as he screamed.

"Do you have any idea what Jerry Lewis did to this script when he got his hands on it? Any fucking idea? It's an important story and it needs to be told the way it was originally written and I've got Chevy Chase interested in it and you have *no! fucking!! right!!!*"

This was the one point in the conversation where I became truly terrified. Not of him. I was terrified of suddenly exploding with laughter, right in his face, and causing him to turn into a Pillar of Roaring, Sentient Wheatgrass and strangle me.

Chevy Chase. In clown makeup. In Auschwitz. I

wanted, more than anything in the world, to see that film. If my shutting down my reading could do anything toward helping that become a reality, I felt like it was my cosmic duty to man up and disappoint my audience.

The Would-Be Producer and his bulging neck veins stomped back to his Volvo and screeched away, after I assured him that not a single word of the bastardized miracle that was *The Day the Clown Cried* would be uttered by my hopeless company of nobodies. And I also promised him I would never never never do anything like this again in Los Angeles, cross my heart and hope to die. This seemed to placate him, and his reminding me, again, that he'd hosted a party at Sundance for six hundred people seemed to calm him down even more.

The sun was setting and the audience was settling in. I walked back into the theater, giddy and depressed.

I was giddy about the whole Chevy Chase/clown makeup/Auschwitz thing. I was depressed for two reasons. The first being that I realized it wasn't Jerry Lewis who had presented the cease-and-desist. It was this beautiful, bellowing bozo who truly believed this was a Script That Must Be Filmed. I was also disappointed in myself, for making the internal decision to agree to his demands. I was cringing at how I was going to break the news to the cast. But this was outside the mere sphere of my own honor and stature. The Powerhouse Theatre was in jeopardy, along with the owner. What was it that Stephen King wrote, near the end of his novella *The Body*? If you die alone, you're a hero. Take anyone with you, you're dog shit. I was feeling the same way, at the moment, about legal action.

So I lowered the boom on the cast. There was frustration, and amusement, and some quick haggling as we all figured out what to do. David Cross pointed out that, in their haste and stupidity, they'd cc'd the cease-and-desist letter to Dave Coulier, who was also mentioned in the "Pick of the Week" blurb. We all had a nice laugh over that, but it didn't change my mind.

The lights went down and I stepped out onstage with the cease-and-desist letter in my hand. I explained to the audience what had happened. Boos. Groans. And then, piece by piece, we all improvised an evening around the fact that we'd been canceled. Bob and David improvised their interpretation of exactly what happened when the producer found out about the reading in *LA Weekly* ("How the fuck will anyone go see our movie in Kansas if eight people watch a script reading for free in Santa Monica?"). Paul F. Tompkins did a flawless phone call between the producer of the film and Peter O'Toole, trying to snake the role of the clown away from Jerry Lewis. Toby Huss played a concerned white supremacist who took issue with the screenplay's "negative" depiction of the Third Reich. And then everyone did a massive, free-form, back-and-forth "interpretive dance/pantomime/musical" version of the screenplay. Sloppy, hilarious and impossible to sue. What else could you ask for in an evening of theater?

I stayed true to the promise I gave to Soy Spasm the Producer. I never once did another reading of *The Day the Clown Cried* in Los Angeles. Every other reading I did was in New York. If it makes him feel any better, I tried my best to avoid any C-list entertainers. I hope he considers Stephen Colbert, Will Arnett and Fred Willard at least B-list. I mean, they're no Chevy Chase . . .

- - - - -

Postscript: I didn't write down the exact date. I must have been too stunned, when it happened, to remember to write it down. But the year after the Powerhouse Theatre disaster, I came within ten feet of *The Day the Clown Cried.*

At least, I think I did.

It was early August 1998. Henny Youngman died in February of that year. I and about a dozen other comedians were brought to the CBS Television City studios, weeks before the Muscular Dystrophy Association Labor Day telethon. Jerry Lewis had an idea—have a group of young comedians come out, during the telethon, and each perform one of Henny's signature one-liners.

I can't tell you who else was in that room, meeting with Jerry, discussing the idea. For one, *Jerry fucking Lewis* was sitting there. I said hello briefly and that was it, as far as our interacting.

The second reason I can't tell you who else was in that room besides me and Jerry was the fact that a silvery, bulletproof-looking briefcase was sitting on Jerry's desk, between Jerry and me. And urban legend had it that Jerry carried the print—or at least a videotape—of *The Day the Clown Cried* with him, at all times, in a big, bulletproof briefcase.

And there it was. As far as I knew.

131

Jerry had us each do a one-liner and it was clear, almost instantly, that this was a bad idea.

But I could not take my eyes off of that briefcase. What if something in my brain fritzed out, some politeness firewall crumbled and burst, and I grabbed the briefcase and ran? Fled into the city, with whatever minions Jerry Lewis could muster scouring the earth searching for me? Would the videotape even be in there? Could I get to a pair of VCRs in time to make a dub, to send it out into the world? What would happen if I did?

I stood, frozen. After the last comedian did a Youngman joke, Jerry's assistant thanked us, wished us a pleasant day and, through tone and stance alone, sent us out of the room. I looked at the briefcase one last time. Then at Jerry. He looked back at me—right into my eyes—but betrayed nothing. Did his eyes say nothing because there was nothing to say? Or was it a trained response, a defense built up after years of guarding his terrible, forbidden prize?

It's my briefcase–from–*Pulp Fiction* moment. Occasionally, in my dreams, I pop the lid on that case and a rebuking, Ark of the Covenant, Nazi-melting glow bursts from its maw and turns me into soggy, goy ashes. Other times, there's a returned letter from Dean Martin and a bottle of Ensure. Each possibility holds secrets and terrors.

Amsterdam

January 7–13, 1998

FEBRUARY SUN MON TUE WED THU FRI SAT 1 2 3 4 5 6 7 8 9 10 11 12 13 14 15 16 17 18 19 20 21 22 23 24 25 26 27 28	~~JANUARY HAPPENING~~ 8pm James N. Bundy ✓ **1** S.F. 4:10 pm FLT 2437 BUR 5:16 pm ✓ NEW YEAR'S DAY	**2**
7 ●—————	—Toomler **8** Amsterdam	**9** —————
14	IMPROV **15** Irvine ✓	**16** WAG KE DOG Los Feliz 3 ✓
GOOD WILL HUNTING Galaxy ✓ **21** SUPER NERDS: DUNGEON PLANET ✓	**22** ●—————	—Seattle— **23** Comedy Underground

I was standing inside the Van Gogh Museum on January 11—a gray, rainy Sunday. And I was crying my eyes out.

Not because I'd been let go by *MADtv*. And not because their decision was right. No one gives a shit if you can point out that a sketch idea was already done by *Saturday Night Live* or *Monty Python* if you don't have a better suggestion. It also didn't help that my writing at the time was so fashionably half-assed. I hadn't even developed my distaste for typos, which made all the sketches I turned in look like I'd written them while being chased by Turkish assassins on a drifting steamboat.

I also wasn't sad because my comedy wasn't going over well in Amsterdam. I'd been booked there for a week at a club called Toomler. Me and Louie CK. Louie was head-lining and absolutely killing. His ideas were huge and his delivery was simple. I was still in that awkward stage where my ideas were simpler and less startling than I cared to admit, so I masked that with a lot of unnecessarily ornate vocabulary and dense cultural references. The audiences were very . . . *polite* to me.

I didn't do myself any favors by making a beeline for Amsterdam's pot-friendly "coffee shops" and inhaling lungfuls of White Widow, Abraxas and Deep Purple every morning with my coffee, orange juice and croissants. After one afternoon spent at a shop called Lucky Mothers, where they packed three joints' worth of high-octane weed into a Snickers bar, which I promptly ate while walking around, I did an entire set of comedy with my eyes closed. The pot didn't affect my diction or lucidity. I could speak clearly. I knew the order of all of my jokes. I could deliver everything perfectly and professionally. But I could not *physically keep my eyes open*. The audience didn't seem at all shocked. They'd seen smacked-assed young Americans before. And watching me deliver jokes with my eyelids firmly snapped shut ended up being way more entertaining than the actual jokes.

I was crying because I was looking at, essentially, a collection of self-portraits that van Gogh and his circle of then-friends—Gauguin included—had done of each other and then exchanged, "Secret Santa" style, one Christmas when they were broke and unable to buy each other presents.

It was one of the many times I've been completely, from-the-ground-up wrong about how I saw the world and my assumptions about how to live in it. In that moment, looking at all of those little self-portraits, exchanged by a circle of friends to make a poverty-level Christmas bearable, all of my beacons were scrambled.

Van Gogh did have true, crackling genius inside of him. But it didn't save him, and despite what I always believed about how absolute geniuses must view the world and move through it, unencumbered by sentiment or responsibility, van Gogh didn't look to his genius to save him. He wanted to live in—and be saved by—the world.

The man who tore *The Night Café* from the boarded basement of his subconscious also organized a simple, prosaic gift exchange among his friends. So he and his friends could have a Christmas. So the world they lived in could seem a little less dim, cold and bleak. *The Night Café* and Secret Santa. I can never know for sure, but I'll bet the inspiration about the gifting of the self-portraits pleased and comforted him far more than *The Night Café* ever could.

What the fuck was I doing? I'd been in Amsterdam almost a week, and despite spending most mornings walking around and seeing the chess clubs, museums, red-light districts, Anne Frank House and pot cafés, I was also spending a good portion of my afternoons holed up in my hotel room, devouring Criterion Collection DVDs.

I Know Where I'm Going!, *Ali: Fear Eats the Soul* and Hiroshi Inagaki's *Samurai Trilogy*. Hoping for some sort of frisson of madness to unlock . . . something. What? Some hidden Key to Directing that needed to be teased out of my head? I was traveling with Louie CK—a stand-up on his way to becoming a filmmaker by simply shooting film. I'd probably watched three times the amount of films that guy had seen, so far, in his life. But I hadn't shot one frame of celluloid.

One afternoon Louie and I went walking, randomly, through the north part of the city. We found a basement chess club. Nothing formal. Card tables set up. Old men slapping pieces onto cheap chessboards. Cigarette smoke. Strong tea in plastic cups. A woman in the back with a sandwich press. You want a ham and cheese? Two guilders. You only have one? Fine, one. Here's your sandwich.

Paperbacks with no covers, ancient magazines. Cats curled up in the window. At three o'clock, with no warning, the owner suddenly shooed everyone out.

"Closing. We have to close. I remembered a thing I have to do." Unsmiling, but weirdly polite. It was how his day was going. Everyone should have been happy for the few hours he was open.

Walking away, Louie said, "That'd be a good place to end up. A good life to have."

"What, running a chess club?"

Louie said, "He doesn't exactly run it. He just really likes chess, so he found a little space where some of his friends, and random people like us, can come by and play. Maybe have a sandwich, some tea. That's a peaceful life."

I said, "Probably doesn't have to answer to anyone."

"Opens and closes when he wants."

I said, "I wonder, then, back in the States? When you see some little, I don't know, model train shop? Or candle store or used bookstore? I wonder how many foreign travelers have stepped into those places and thought the same thing we're thinking now, about that chess club."

Louie said, "Well, yeah. We see that stuff every day in our lives, and we don't think twice about it. But you see it in a foreign country and it makes you rethink your life."

That conversation stayed with me, always. Mainly for its own merits. But, years later, when Louie got his show on FX? That brilliant, one-of-a-kind show he does at his own pace, with no notes, in a small way for zero money because he loves writing and acting and directing, and also showcasing his funny friends? He finally got his Amsterdam chess club.

I remember another conversation with Louie, during after-show drinks, when he waxed horrific and hilarious about tourism:

"One way to do a city like this would be to put your passport and a change of clean clothes and a wad of money in a safe-deposit box. Or a locker at a train station, right? And you leave the key with someone you trust, who'll know where you are. And then you go out and eat the city whole. All the booze you want, pot, any pills that get thrown at you, anything sexually, stuff you can't even remember. And you know you've got this escape hatch in a little storage locker somewhere. And you can scrub off anything you do to yourself for a twenty-four-hour period. Either a city like this, or maybe somewhere in Thailand or Jamaica."

I'm waiting to see what that TV show's going to be.

Then we visited the Rijksmuseum and viewed Rembrandt's *The Night Watch*. The painting had been slashed with a shoemaker's knife in 1911, and again in 1975 (this time with a bread knife, leaving massive, still-visible scars) and, finally, eight years before our visit, by an acid-throwing maniac. More madness, this time surrounding a painting depicting, at least in its action, law and order shining a beam through the darkness.

And how was the museum protecting this dark star of a canvas from future attacks? A single velvet rope between two stanchions, a nearby fire extinguisher and a sleepy, septuagenarian security guard.

"That probably includes a lunch break for the guard," said Louie.

■ ■ ■ ■ ■

So there I was, my second-to-last day in Amsterdam, alone inside the Van Gogh Museum, getting kicked in the head. Gently. Again. Unlike the movies, where Our Hero suddenly has some massive revelation and becomes a New Person instantly, the true road out of a rut consists of a bunch of small, sharp kicks. Here was one small kick—crying in public, thinking of Vincent, clinging to the cliff-edge of friendship, and peace, and happiness, and being pulled down by a demon with paint-gob eyes and streaked, blazing claws of color.

Other kicks were piling up. The Hammer Studios marathon. And my trip back to Virginia for Thanksgiving. *The Day the Clown Cried* debacle at the Powerhouse Theatre. And now this. I'm embarrassed to say it, but looking at those little self-portraits? I thought of a line from *Apocalypse Now*. When Dennis Hopper is describing Marlon Brando's Colonel Kurtz:

"The man is clear in his mind. But his soul is mad."

And I still had a year and a half to go before the final kick that launched me out of my movie-watching madness.

CHAPTER TEN

The Knave of Queens

March 26–27, 1998

11	12	13	14
FERNWOOD 2NIGHT @ the DGA ✓	IMPROV ✓	IMPROV ✓	WACO: RULES of ENGAGEMENT Sunset 5 ✓ MEAN STREETS NuArt ✓
18 TRACKDOWN HOUSE: STRAIGHT, NO CHASER N. Beverly ✓ VELVEETA UNDERGROUND ✓	**19** LET'S GET LOST N. Beverly ✓	**20** MR. NICE GUY Chinese/Cinerama ✓ WILD THINGS Galaxy ✓	**21** THE PRODUCERS & IT'S A MAD, MAD, MAD, MAD WORLD N. Beverly ✓ HOLLYWOOD COFFEE SHOP ✓
25 LUNA PARK ✓ "Stella"	**26** TOOL @ the PALLADIUM ✓	**27** "KING OF QUEENS" pilot taping Sony/Columbia ✓	**28** JAMES ELLROY: DEMON DOG OF AMERICAN FICTION NuArt ✓

Movie-wise, March of 1998 was looking like a champion. I started the month seeing *Dark City* in Toronto, then went back to Los Angeles for a gorgeous print of *Les Enfants du Paradis* at the New Beverly. And then, of course, *The Big Lebowski*. Endless night, battered hope and bowling noir. Nice beginning.

The month ended surreal.

I saw *The Big Lebowski* in Sherman Oaks on Friday, March 6. Brian Posehn and I went, fresh off the plane from Portland, Oregon, where we'd spent four days writing the pilot script for *Super Nerds*, which Comedy Central would shoot and then bury in a salt mine somewhere in Colorado. Oh well.

We spent the next day in a studio somewhere on the outskirts of Silver Lake, dressed as hookers and being filmed by Maynard Keenan for a video. His band, Tool, had a song called "Hooker with a Penis" and he wanted footage of shadowy, man-shaped but ostensibly female dancers to be projected behind him when they performed at the Palladium on March 26. He asked us. We are tragically, hopelessly man-shaped, Brian and I. So we squeezed into garters and nighties, threw boas around our necks and danced for the cameras. Our silhouettes were captured for eternity. Maynard and his crew took some still photographs of our journey into half-assed cross-dressing. At one goofy juncture, I sat on the toilet and pretended to wipe my crotch with a wad of toilet paper while scowling from under the curly bangs of a black wig. Snap! Comedy!

The night of the concert I was sober and looking to go home early. The next day, Friday the twenty-seventh, I was set to tape the pilot of *The King of Queens*. All the way out at Sony, in Culver City. I was ambivalent about the pilot and frustrated at the concert about having to stay sober. I liked getting a solid buzz at a show and letting the sonic surge scrape my frontal lobes. Tool, live, is a full-body scour.

I could have used the scour, too. The rest of the month, film-wise, had gotten relentless and heavy. *Hidden Fear* (repressed, late-fifties noir, set in Denmark [!]), then the documentary *Waco: The Rules of Engagement* (burned babies), then *Mean Streets* ("You don't fuck with the infinite"), John Sayles's *Men with Guns* (the grinding hopelessness and sudden blood under eco-friendly tourism) and finally *Thelonious Monk: Straight, No Chaser* (more genius at the price of madness).

But there I was, in the balcony, watching my and Brian's shadows writhing clumsily behind Maynard and Tool as they stutter-stomped through "Hooker with a Penis." They segued into "Sober" and then Brian came up behind me.

"Check out the tour T-shirt," he said, laughing.

Black tee. An image on the front—grainy, me on the toilet, clutching the toilet paper wad. Scowling at the lens. And around the image, in a circle, was: "*Tool Fucked the Shit out of Me at the Palladium and All I Got Was This Lousy T-shirt.*"

"Wow!" I said. "That's fantastic! Oh man, he didn't tell me he was going to do *that*." I ran and bought five of them.

The *King of Queens* pilot taping went until three a.m. on the twenty-eighth. At one point me, Kevin James, Victor Williams and Larry Romano are all piled onto Doug's bed, trying to watch a football game on Doug's big-screen TV. In between takes I lay down on the bed and fell instantly asleep. I dreamed a very prosaic, undreamy dream about being back in my apartment. When they called for the next shot I snapped awake and didn't know where I was. It was the kind of panic I used to get when I'd wake up after a Norse-warrior night of drinking, only I was stone sober and lying safe on a frilly bed on a soundstage.

The day before I had been a forty-foot silhouette of a she-male behind Tool at the Palladium. My face was on a T-shirt that extolled rough group sex. Now I was taping the pilot for an eight p.m., Monday night sitcom that would be my main source of employment for the next nine years. It bought me a house. It bought me breathing room and the ability to fill comedy clubs and small theaters. I learned to act, literally, by getting to work with Kevin James every day. He was the most solid TV actor I've ever seen since Danny DeVito and, before Danny, Jackie Gleason. Those are rare birds, with the ability to rampage with movie-star bluster inside of a TV-screen playing field.

And I could not have had a more solid demarcation line between my young, pissed-off "alt comic" years and my mellowing, mainstream acting years. Being a hooker with a penis for Tool the night before my *King of Queens* pilot taping is my reverse "Goodbye Yellow Brick Road." But the lure of television, especially for people outside of it, is a more sinister tractor beam pull than the distant, emerald glow of Oz. Within a year, I'd find out exactly how sinister that pull was, and how warping to a seemingly sane psyche.

CHAPTER ELEVEN

Killer Burger and the Myth of the Largo

March 4–20, 1999

10 69/296	11 70/295	12 71/294	13 72/293
		"KING of QUEENS" taping ✓	
17 76/289 St. Patrick's Day (Ireland, US) The BRANDON TEENS Story NuArt ✓	18 77/288	19 78/287	20 79/286 KILLER BURGER ✓
24 83/282 COBB'S ✓ SHADOW of a DOUBT Castro ✓	25 84/281 LENNY BRUCE: SWEAR to tell the TRUTH Roxie → PUNCHLINE	26 85/280 S.F. ED TV Empire ✓	27 86/279 ✓ RAVENOUS Roxie II ✓

"Hey, long time no see!"

I'm finishing a set at a Borders bookstore. It's the Borders that used to be perched above the intersection of La Cienega and Blackburn. As I'm writing this it's a Men's Wearhouse. By the time you're reading this it might be a Chipotle. Welcome to Los Angeles.

It's March, 4, 1999. I'm filming episodes of *The King of Queens*, getting used to being on TV. Just like when I was at *MADtv*, I'm doing sets ferociously. Almost every night, except for the ones where I huddle in a seat at the New Beverly.

The Largo is at the peak of its popularity and influence. I do regular Monday night sets there. But I make sure to seek out odder, on-the-fringes rooms. Rooms where you have to *work*. Like this Borders, where a friend of mine puts on a regular Thursday night show in the upstairs Borders Café. The crowd is ideal if you're in the mood to work out. Half of them are there to actually see the show; the other half just want to sit and read, and you have to win them over. Oftentimes, the half that was there to see comedy ends up agreeing with the oblivious half. It's pitiless and perfect.

I come offstage. Wait, no. There isn't a stage. I've stepped away from the spot they cleared in one corner of the café area, away from the mike and back toward the shelves of books. I judge the set successful because, after one joke, an Asian girl who was reading John Grisham's *The Runaway Jury* looked up and halfheartedly smiled at me. And then went back to her book.

I don't recognize, at first, the man who walks up to me. He says, "Hey, long time no see!" Brown haired, slightly older than me, average-by-way-of-pleasant-looking. Solid, Midwestern breeding. Like he's stepped out of one of those stock photo images you see in magazine ads for dress slacks. "Not since Richmond, right?"

And then it comes flooding back to me.

Before we proceed, I've got to tell you that I'm not going to name the guy. He doesn't come off well in this story. And he isn't a bad guy. *Misguided* is a better word.

But for the purposes of this chapter, let's call him Ted. Ted Richmond. *Ted* because, well—is there any more average-by-way-of-pleasant name than *Ted*? And *Richmond* because I've realized that Richmond was the last place I saw him.

It was back in 1991, just before I moved west. The spring. I was still in college, getting ready to graduate. My senior year of college was an epic struggle for me. I realized, halfway through my junior year, that all I wanted to do with my life was become a stand-up comedian. So my senior year of college was a live-action version of those high school anxiety dreams. You know the ones, where you're not ready for some huge test, but you're also vaguely aware of the life you're living now, and of the knowledge and wisdom you've accrued through your life, and how you *do not belong back in high school anymore* but—you're trapped! You're *trapped*! How did it get like this? Don't they realize you already graduated?

Every Wednesday, those last two years of college, I hosted an open mike at a local comedy club, there in my college town. There was a regular circle of comedians I hung out with way more than my college friends. Every weekend I was away, working a gig. I knew what I wanted to do.

Ted Richmond was a regular at the Wednesday night open mike. And of all the regular comedians on that show, he was far and away my favorite. He had a truly original, bizarre, oblique approach to jokes. Sometimes the punch lines were hidden in the middle. Sometimes the setup was the punch line, in that it was so startling, so confusing, that he'd follow it, masterfully, with everyday observations, to give the audience time to let the crust-shifting, plangent thought sink in. He did okay with audiences but amazing with every other comedian. A true original, I thought, with an unhurried, confident, long-view approach to his art and career.

"They say we're going to know the devil by his number, 666," began one of Ted's bits. Then he'd say, "Aren't we going to know him by the fact he's the only one with a *number*? What does 666 have to do with it? 'What's your number? Six sixty-four? How about you? Six sixty-five? Okay . . .

"And you? Six six six? Okey-doke. Six six six, come over here for a second."

Laconic, weird, playful. Brilliant.

We were acquaintances. He was always friendly but never particularly close to anyone. A true lovable oddball. I moved west and never heard from him.

For a short time.

And then . . .

Starting in 1994, he'd call me. Always at weird, random hours, when I wasn't picking up my phone. At first he'd call the number in my apartment. Someone I knew on the East Coast must have given it to him. After I got a cell phone, he began calling that. But, as if he had some eerie sixth sense, never when I was there to answer. Always wanting to talk, yet never *once* leaving a number at which to return his calls. I think at one point, when I was back visiting the East Coast, I ran into a mutual friend from those open-mike days at my college.

"Hey, do you keep up with Ted Richmond at all?"

My East Coast friend said, "Yeah. He lives in New York now, but I see him sometimes."

I asked, "Do you have his phone number?"

"Not on me."

I said, "Well, when you see him, tell him to call me and leave a number where I can call him back. He's left me ten messages over these last few years, and I think he thinks I have his number, but I don't, and I feel like I'm being rude."

"You got it," said my friend.

A week later, on my answering machine, a call from Ted. He left it at three o'clock in the morning, West Coast time. His flat, pleasant, slightly spacey voice was on the tape, like a stoned ghost:

"Hey, Patton. Ted. Giving you a call. I was told you've been trying to call me back. Well, nothing's stopping you. Give me a call." *Click*. Goddamn it.

And now, here he is. In the flesh.

"Do you know how many times I wanted to call you back? You never left a number!" I say, shaking my head.

"I didn't? I always left messages on your machine."

I say, "Yeah, but you've got to *say* what your phone number is. It doesn't just leave it on the machine, you know? That's why I couldn't call you back. I hope you weren't pissed off."

Ted says, "Nah, I figured you were just getting around to it." In Ted's mind, a three-year lapse is a perfectly acceptable, on-pace lag for returning a phone call.

"So what're you doing in Los Angeles? You move here?"

Ted smiles. "Thinking of it. Thinking real hard about it. Want to do some stand-up."

I say, "Oh, cool! Right now you can pretty much go onstage every night. There are all of these amazing—"

"Largo."

Something in his tone catches me short. His eyes, which were always twinkling with the slightly unhinged genius you see in people like Andy Kaufman or Maria Bamford, have suddenly gone dead. Dead, but still hungry, which doesn't fit his face. Shark eyes in a teddy bear skull.

"Well, the Largo's a great room, but you don't want to just—"

Ted cuts me off again. "The Largo. I want to go up at the Largo and do a set and have a TV show. I read about that place. In *Rolling Stone*. There are TV people there and you go onstage and you get a show."

I say, "Hey, whoa. It's not exactly like that. The room's really popular, but it's not like you do one set and suddenly you're on TV."

"Well, *you're* on TV. And you do the Largo."

Okay, let's stop here for a second. Because I don't want you thinking this is a Country Mouse/City Mouse story where I suddenly have to contend with a misinformed yokel who's putting his misperceptions about show business and Life in the Big City on me, and I have to avoid him and find a way to extract him from my life. I like this guy. And he's no fool. He is, objectively, one of the more original comedic minds I've ever encountered. It's true that some of the full-goose creative types can be a little . . . shaky, when it comes to quotidian life, but Ted is far from that. And he isn't like some other friends of mine from back home. Like the high school friend who called me after my single line of dialogue on the "Couch" episode of *Seinfeld*, demanding I let him live in the guest house of my "mansion" while he started learning to "act for the movies." When I assured him that I didn't have a house, that I still lived in an efficiency apartment in Little Armenia, he countered with, "I saw you on TV. You don't think I have a TV? You're a millionaire. *I saw you on TV.*" When I explained that I'd gotten a little over four hundred dollars for my acting services on *Seinfeld*, he hung up on me and told everyone I still knew back home that I'd turned into a "Hollywood asshole."

But Ted isn't like that. Or so I think. And I am well and truly his fan, and I guess I think I'm his friend, as far as that's possible with someone like Ted.

"Look, you don't want to just go up at the Largo just like that. Let me take you to a few of the smaller rooms. They're all amazing. I want you to have a feel for how stand-up is out here, and then, yeah, I'll definitely get you up at the Largo."

Ted scowls at me. "I read about that place. You go up and you get a show. And you're trying to keep me from going on there and you're already on TV and I don't have *time* to do these little rooms."

Now I'm starting to doubt myself. Am I being an asshole to him?

●●●●●

Sixteen days later we're in the cramped back room of a Hollywood Boulevard restaurant called Killer Burger. There's a Saturday night open mike hosted by Jeremy Kramer, about whom a better writer than me needs to compose a sprawling, Robert Caro–sized biography. To the alternate comedy scene, he is Johnny Cash, Joey Ramone and Bo Diddley. The three-in-one. The Rosetta stone. Too big for my head, too wild for my pen.

Anyway.

So I've brought Ted here to do a set. It's a tiny room that's gotten a lot of heat. Mainly because of Jeremy. Jeremy does the sort of free-form, fearless, nonlinear humor that Ted does. I figure they're a perfect match, that Jeremy will set the table for him, then Ted can go up, do a set where it doesn't matter how good or bad he does. What kind of friend would I be if I simply tossed him onto the Largo? In the sixteen days leading up to the Killer Burger show, I've learned from him that he's never even been to the Largo or seen a show there. He read an article, formed a myth and is proceeding as if the myth were gospel.

Then I find out something else, something even more frustrating and exasperating, while he waits to go on.

"How long were you living in New York?"

Ted says, "About a month."

"A month in the city? In Manhattan?" I'm confused. "Where did you end up living?"

Ted says, "Upstate."

"Huh." I think about this. Then: "Where'd you do sets?"

Ted stares at me. "I didn't like Manhattan. I didn't do any sets there. I painted houses upstate."

"Was there a club upstate?"

Ted thinks about this for a second. "I don't think I've done comedy in, um. Um. Eight years."

Now it's my turn to stare. "You haven't done *any* stand-up. In eight years."

"Nope." He grins. "There really weren't any rooms to work out in upstate. And like I said, I hated Manhattan."

He hasn't been onstage in eight fucking years. Holy shit.

"Why . . . I mean, why are you suddenly wanting to do comedy now?"

Ted says, confidently, "To go onstage at the Largo. And get a TV show."

Ten minutes later, Jeremy brings Ted onstage.

I really, really, really want to tell you a victorious, Geoffrey Rush–in–*Shine* tale of victory here. But even though that movie is based on a true story, it's still a fucking movie. And there's nothing cinematic about Ted's set at the Killer Burger that night.

Jeremy gives him a nice intro. Straight up. "Ladies and gentlemen, from New York, please welcome Ted Richmond."

Ted walks up, holds on to the mike stand with both hands. Looks at Jeremy. "I'm from New York State. You made it sound like I'm from New York City. I don't live there now."

Jeremy says, from his seat, "Ladies and gentlemen, from the *state* of New York but not the city, Ted Richmond." He's being playful, but with a solid undercurrent of *Let's not fuck with me, okay?*

Ted glares back at him. "New York *state*."

"I said that," says Jeremy.

"Not originally."

Jeremy says, "We should move on."

Ted keeps staring at Jeremy. The audience is getting uncomfortable.

What follows is eight minutes of . . . look, someone who didn't know comedy would call it "hate-fucking a crowd." But there's no malice to it. Which makes it even more disturbing. A complete emotional disconnect as he delivers half concepts ("Everyone's mad that the president is lying to us. But he's talking to us. And *we* lie. And *we* don't talk to the president") and apologies before an attempt at humor was ever gambled ("I don't want to talk about the next thing that's in my head to talk about, because you won't want to hear me say it"). Stone-silent crowd. Ted walks off without saying good night. Midsentence. Simply stops talking and walks off the stage.

I meet him in the front restaurant. I try to be supportive.

"Old muscles, huh? But they come back, right?"

Ted says, "That sucked."

"Well, aren't you glad your first set in eight years wasn't at the Largo?"

Ted considers this. "I wouldn't have done that shit at the Largo. I would've done my best stuff and then gotten a TV show. None of those people in there could have given me a TV show."

I don't know what to say. To be honest, I feel like if I open my mouth, say anything, he'll flat-out kill me.

Ted turns and walks out of Killer Burger and, as far as I know, off of the planet.

He says over his shoulder as he heads for the door, "You're on TV and you won't let me on. No one will let me on TV."

He disappears into the flow of pedestrians on Hollywood Boulevard. A random electron in Los Angeles's ever-crackling circuit of need and delusion. I never see him again.

CHAPTER TWELVE

The End of the Addiction

Thursday, May 20, 1999, the Vista Theatre

Sherman Torgan

Courtesy of Michael Torgan

So now it's four years, to the day, since I first stepped inside the New Beverly. Stepped out of May sunshine to watch Billy Wilder noir. Billy Wilder—a double dose. *Sunset Boulevard* and *Ace in the Hole*. Billy Wilder stuck the needle in. Four years later, George Lucas yanks the needle out.

I see *The Phantom Menace*. Midnight screening at the Vista Theatre, Wednesday the nineteenth, at Hillhurst where it crazy-collides with Sunset and Hollywood. Gorgeous, old-school, art deco theater with extra-wide aisles, a movie palace interior and a manager—Victor—who often dresses up like characters in the movie they're showing. Victor is, and will continue to be, a friend. He gets me and two other friends into the midnight screening. I've waited since 1983, when I saw *Return of the Jedi* at the Tysons Corner 8 in Fairfax, Virginia, for another chapter of the *Star Wars* saga.

There's no point in my plumbing the depths of the disappointment I feel, later, trudging out of the Vista at two a.m. the morning of the twentieth. How do I put it? There've been so many metaphors, at this point.

My favorite, so far, is from comedian Dana Gould: "George Lucas told the greatest joke about two men walking into a bar in 1977. Now, twenty-two years later, it's time to find out how the bar got its zoning permits, and liquor license, and how they hired the busboy."

But since I feel obligated to put *something* of my own here, even after all of the jaw flapping I've done about it, how about . . . Okay, think of it this way. Imagine that all four members of Led Zeppelin are still alive. And they're doing a reunion show. And you get there, and it turns out that Robert Plant has fired the other three members, and he's hired three frightened music students and is insisting they perform acoustic versions of the chord progressions that led to songs like "Black Dog" and "Whole Lotta Love."

Eh. Still not as good as Dana. Here's another one, from my own brother, who sat next to me, during one of the Galactic Senate scenes:

"This is like watching C-SPAN but everyone's wearing monster masks."

But two things happen, a week after I leave that screening.

First off, let me fully admit to seeing *The Phantom Menace* again, that Saturday, at the now-defunct Coronet Theatre on Geary in San Francisco. I'm doing a weekend there at Cobb's Comedy Club, and I guess I'm hoping for some sort of redemptive miracle, or that maybe I was wrong in my initial assessment. Also, there are parts of it I like. It's sheer, uncut nostalgia. I want to see a *Star Wars* movie in a theater with a lot of people. Like I did when I was eight, and had my mind blown apart.

But it still sucks.

And then—the Two Things. These two things are what pull the needle out of my cinephilia, for good. They peel me forever from the projector sprockets. I still haven't directed a film, but films don't direct my life, either. So that's something.

The first thing that happens is: I go back to the New Beverly the Sunday I return from San Francisco. They're showing *Only Angels Have Wings* and *His Girl Friday*. Howard Hawks and Cary Grant. Two films about two different professions (bush pilots and newspapermen) with slangy secret languages and ethics that seem brutal and heartless to outsiders. Come to think of it, those two films go farther than pretty much any other movie in explaining the codes and rituals of comedians. If the second chapter of this book doesn't explain my world to you, go watch those two movies instead.

I buy my ticket and Sherman looks at me through the glass with his merry, camera-lens eyes.

"Patton."

I say, "Hey, Sherman."

"Four years to the day. Figured you'd be handing me a script to read by now."

(*Kick.*)

Then, a week later, I have dinner with some other movie-buff friends, all of us steeped in the *Star Wars* universe. And—and I remember so much of this conversation—we pick apart *The Phantom Menace*. We aren't happy with it.

But we also have very detailed, very reasonable, *very* personal reasons for believing the film could have been better. And not only better, but great. As thrilling as *Star Wars*, as deep and dark as *Empire* and as satisfying as *Jedi*.

Why is our conversation so detailed, so astute, so passionate? Well, part of it is we're sprocket fiends, film freaks, with one foot always in the celluloid world. That would always be a fact.

But the other reason is: George Lucas created something that, even when it makes a wrong turn, has a rich enough history to it, and has enough life pulsing through its heart, that we could have conversations like this. And arguments. Classic films that are better regarded than *Star Wars* rarely spawn an entire subculture of argument, speculation and even greater creativity. And I'm not even talking fan fiction. I'm talking about other short films, gorgeous YouTube spoofs like *Troops* or *Stabbing at Leia's 22nd Birthday.** Websites that make intricate, detailed short films about *The Phantom Menace* and the subsequent, even more disappointing prequels, with anguished, often brilliant ideas on how to improve them. Like *The Godfather: Part III*, which is a stunted flower growing on the rich loam of *The Godfather Parts 1* and *2*. I still have friends who've posited brilliant alternate versions of the third part of Coppola's trilogy. About how it could have been a war for control between Michael and Tom Hagen. Or how Connie Corleone could have been a hidden puppet master, like Maerose Prizzi in *Prizzi's Honor*. David Thomson, in his brilliant *Suspects* essays, constructed a grand, epic narrative wherein Connie, Maerose and Elvira Montana—Michelle Pfeiffer's character in *Scarface*—form a tripartite drug kingdom.

Movies—the truly great ones (and sometimes the truly bad)—should be a drop in the overall fuel formula for your life. A fuel that should include sex and love and food and movement and friendships and your own work. All of it, feeding the engine. But the engine of your life should be your *life*. And it hits me, sitting there with my friends, that for all of our bluster and detailed, exotic knowledge *about* film, we aren't contributing anything *to* film.

I flash to the coffee shop in San Francisco that all of my comedian friends and I would hang out in, when we were young, before we'd done anything in the way of television or movies. Bitching about how awful and shitty the indus-

---

*Written and directed by Josh Trank, who edited *Big Fan*, my first lead dramatic role in a movie, ten years later.

try was. We were very comfortable, waking up at eleven in the morning, choking down caffeinated mud, assuring ourselves that some invisible foot was keeping us down. Some of us moved to Los Angeles, made our lives. But some of us stayed in that coffee shop, because that's ultimately where our comfort was. There was comfort in preemptive disappointment. Because it was never your fault.

(*Kick.*)

And then, once the group of us who moved down to Los Angeles got there, there was more bitching—about not getting bigger roles or better opportunities to pitch shows for ourselves. And we'd piss and moan and get comfortable—fuck, some of us built whole careers—pointing out how unfair and whimsical and chaotic the entertainment business was, how it rarely rewarded the truly talented. None of us could see how it never rewarded the inert.

(*Kick.*)

And here I am. I've traded a late-morning coffee shop for a late-night, postscreening bar, angry at George Lucas for producing something that doesn't live up to my exacting, demanding, ultimately nonparticipating standards, and failing to see that the four hours of pontificating and connecting and correcting his work could be spent creating two or three pages of my own.

(*KICK KICK KICK.*)

I still haven't made a film. As I write this, I'm fourteen years removed from that flurry of figurative head kicks. But I've written six screenplays. Sold three of them. Have seen none of them made. They're just bigger open mikes for me.

Film stock and movie theaters are dying as I write this, but I've got a phone in my pocket with a mini movie studio inside that I'm learning to use. The Five Books are all gone—hauled away to Goodwill. Maybe you'll find one, with my tight, OCD pencil scrawl next to dozens of movie titles. My movie-a-night habit is gone. And, as I've been cramming fewer films into my head, my memory has opened up and brought into sharper focus moments in films that pierced me, that will stay with me without my ever having to draw a star or check mark next to a title. And for every one of those moments that another human, in a collaborative fit of struggle or passion, brought into being, I'm more attuned to moments in my everyday life— with friends and family and even (sometimes especially) strangers. Faces are scenes. People are films.

. . . *Kick* . . .

Sherman Torgan and George Lucas pulled me off of the sprockets. My love of watching movies has turned into a love of savoring them. And the flirtation with becoming a filmmaker abides, and has stayed fun.

Listen—you don't *have* to follow me into the sunshine. If this is your first time seeing *Sunset Boulevard* and *Ace in the Hole*? By all means sit and see 'em. They're great. I envy your getting to watch them with new eyes. But take what you need from them and get out of the dark once in a while. You're going to have more of the dark than you can handle, sooner than you think.

The thing about the dark is, it can never get enough of you.

Whistling in the Dark

Sherman Torgan died on July 18, 2007. He was riding his bike in Venice Beach when a heart attack toppled him off of the planet and out of this life. Did it look like a scene from a Jacques Tati comedy? Did his life flash before his eyes—and if it did, what movie scenes did it contain? Or had he beat the addiction, too, and was content to lead others into it, hoping for a screenplay from each one, exactly four years after they first entered his celluloid shooting gallery? I'd like to think that Sherman's memory was only enhanced by his years in the darkness, in front of the glowing screen. That the memories of his real life, lit by the cosmic candle of sunlight or deepened by the infinite ink of the evening, were clearer and more precious for his having seen life re-created, secondhand, for so many years watching films.

I was celebrating my nineteenth year, to the day, since I first stepped on a stage the day Sherman passed. I wish I could say I spent it at a club, working on new material. Or even at the New Beverly, watching a Wednesday night double feature and filing away a camera angle, a focus pull or a simple cut as something to emulate and strive for if I ever directed a movie. Instead, I was on a soundstage in Santa Monica, sitting in front of a green screen, running my trap on another episode of VH1's *Best Week Ever*. I was probably mumbling about Paris Hilton or Britney Spears or Some Other Dumb Idiot Whut Was on TV Acting Like an Idiot. Disposable. Rent and ramen on a grander scale.

It was also twenty days after I'd voiced the lead character in Pixar's *Ratatouille*. I was planning on bringing a bottle of "Ratatouille" vintage white wine to Sherman. Pixar and Disney had planned to do a product tie-in but then decided alcohol wasn't appropriate for their young audience. But they sent me one of the bottles, now a near-impossible-to-get collector's item. I don't like accruing artifacts of my career, so I wanted to give it to Sherman. To make up for the screenplay I never handed him through the booth. But now he was gone.

On August 18 there was a sloppy, spontaneously organized "wake" inside the Egyptian Theatre. Everyone who attended had decided, without ever saying it out loud, that it would have been impossible to mourn Sherman inside his own temple. So we met in a theater designed for a pharaoh's farewell journey and told New Beverly stories. I told the one about Laurence Tierney. Clu Gulager, who played the fitness-obsessed hitman in Don Siegel's *The Killers* as well as fighting off a punk-rock ghoul invasion in *Return of the Living Dead*, talked about how going to the New Beverly stopped him from sinking into despair and alcoholism. Julie Marchese, and her bright green Louise Brooks haircut, didn't attend.

The despair was too deep, too fresh for her. She, along with Sherman's son Michael, was about to grab the tiller of the temporarily adrift movie ark that the New Beverly was becoming. A few days later, Quentin Tarantino announced, "As long as I draw breath, the New Beverly will remain open." When film preservation pioneer Henri Langlois died,* thirty years before and an ocean away, his Cinémathèque Française was also kept running. He saved films from being destroyed by Nazis. Sherman saved them from indifference and passive digital downloads. The Nazis were better dressed than the digital pirates.

I told another story at Sherman's wake, besides the Laurence Tierney one. It was this:

On Friday, November 3, 1995—still fresh into my addiction, still going to the New Beverly three or four times a week—I stopped in to see *Casablanca*. I'd actually seen it twice before—once on television, and then at the Alhambra in San Francisco. But I had a free Friday night, and *Casablanca* is a movie that pays increasing dividends every single time you see it. Why not study it when it's twenty feet tall and early December Los Angeles rain is tattooing the roof? What would I see?

It was a medium-sized audience. Some of the usual freaks were there. I was one of the usual freaks, at that point. I was already noting, to myself, that *Casablanca* appeared in both *The Psychotronic Encyclopedia* (because

---

* "He died like an elephant," said one of his friends.

of Peter Lorre) and *Cult Movies* volume 1. This was a well-spent evening.

We got to the point, near the end, where Rick is sending Ilsa off to be with Laszlo. He's regaining his heart by breaking it. About to start the "Here's looking at you, kid . . . ," speech.

He actually got out the words, "The problems of three little people don't amount to a hill of—" and then the word "beans" became warped and shrill and then silent as *the film broke*. The fucking film *broke* right at the moment in *Casablanca* that everyone knows, that everyone can quote, that the whole film leads up to, emotionally!

There was, at most, half a second of outrage, of half-expelled *Wha*s and *Huh*s, and then silence. Stunned. And then . . .

Laughter. From everyone. The house lights went up as Sherman and his projectionist rushed up to the projection room to fix the problem. The light brought more laughter. Of all the places for *Casablanca* to break. It couldn't have been timed more perfectly.

And then the lights went down again. Darkness. Was the movie going to restart? Nope. Not yet. Just sitting there, in the dark. Nothing glowing on the screen.

And then everyone . . .

. . . began . . .

. . . *whistling*.

We all started spontaneously whistling "As Time Goes By," maybe twenty of us, on a rainy Los Angeles evening in the little New Beverly Cinema. Elsewhere in the city people were at nightclubs, seeing concerts, roaring their youth at parties or sporting events. Big movies were premiering to packed houses. Famous comedians were doing sets in crowded clubs. Crimes were being committed, decisions to change one's life were being agreed to. Money changed hands. Rain fell to the earth and made its way back to the sea.

And we were whistling in the dark. "As Time Goes By." You must remember this . . .

I thanked Sherman, apologized for never handing him my screenplay and sat back down in the front row of the Egyptian. Later that week, I stopped by the New Beverly and gave Michael my *Blade Runner* replica gun. It could not have been farther from a finished screenplay, but I needed something symbolic to soothe my self-loathing. The replica gun exchange did it. Barely.

As I write this now, Sherman's been gone for six years. No one's even sure if movie theaters will exist six years from now. Just like when silent movies transitioned to sound, and then black and white to color, and then television appeared, and then videotapes and DVDs. Now there's the Internet, and the ability to pull cinema from an electronic empyrean, to funnel it onto a tiny screen in your pocket. And us sprocket fiends are waiting to see if the movie theaters will continue to stand. We're whistling in the dark. Time is going by.

One thing I didn't talk about at Sherman's wake was a blog I'd written a few weeks after he died. I did it quietly, posted it on my website, used it to vent any residual grief

I was feeling and then didn't think much about it after. I certainly wasn't going to mention a fucking blog inside of a movie palace on Hollywood Boulevard. Why invoke another soldier in the electronic army of distractions that was making it hard on movie theaters?

But I went back and reread it while writing this chapter. It's called "I Will Program a Month in Heaven for You, Sherman Torgan." The second paragraph of that entry, I now realize, was a rough précis of this entire book:

> All I know is, when I moved to Los Angeles in May of 1995, the New Beverly was a cool, dark continent of then-forgotten history. It was Saturday, May 20th—blazing and white outside on Beverly Boulevard. I watched a double feature of *Ace in the Hole* and *Sunset Boulevard. Ace in the Hole* just came out on a deluxe Criterion DVD. Thanks to people like Sherman Torgan, "NOT AVAILABLE ON DVD" will quickly go the way of phrases like, "Who's Michael Reeves?" and "I've never seen *El Topo* or *Blast of Silence*—are they good?"

What I'd done was organize a month's worth of titles to play in a netherworld movie palace. Someplace cool and comfortable, and smelling of popcorn fumes and spilled-soda perfume, where Sherman could unspool heaven.

I've said this elsewhere, but I'm a stone-cold atheist who's genuinely grateful that religion exists. All religions. I look at them as a testament to the human race's imagination, to our ability to invent stories that explain

away—or at least make manageable—the nameless terrors, horrific randomness and utter, galactic meaningless-
ness of the universe. Is there anything more defiant and
beautiful than, when faced with a roaring void, to say, "I
know a story that fits this quite nicely. And I'm going to
use it, pitiless universe, to give meaning and poetry and
hope to my days inside this maelstrom into which I've, in
Joseph Conrad's words, 'blundered unbidden'"?*

None of these movies exist. Well, except for one of
them *definitely* and one of them *maybe*. Some of their
source materials and the actors starring in these films
don't exist in the same time frames. Time and mortality
don't hold sway once you're off this planet. Just like Neil
Gaiman did in the *Brief Lives* story line in his *Sandman*
comics, wherein exists a "dream library" of all the novels that the great writers dreamed of writing but never
did (Chandler's *Love Can Be Murder*, Carroll's *Alice's
Adventures on the Moon*), I dreamed up a cinema where
Sherman could spend the afterlife watching movies that
various great directors dreamed of directing or that the
collective sprocket-fiend consciousness would want to
will into being.

---

*And yes, I'm aware of Conrad's decidedly unatheistic afterthought,
in the very next sentence from this quote: "Or else decoyed." It's from
The Shadow Line. You ought to read it. No need to see the Andrzej
Wajda movie.

August 1 and 2

A Confederacy of Dunces
dir: Hal Ashby
(w/ John Belushi, Richard Pryor and Lily Tomlin)
Blood Meridian
dir: Terrence Malick
(w/ Gene Hackman, Barry Brown
and Marlon Brando)

Hal Ashby and Terrence Malick were at the height of their powers when they each filmed these supposedly "unfilmable" novels.

Ashby refused to "contain" human hurricanes like Belushi and Pryor in his heat-haze adaptation of *Dunces*. Instead, he reportedly played them against each other, expanding the character of Burma Jones from the novel for Pryor to inhabit, and letting Belushi create his own interpretation of Ignatius, which was miraculous for how close it ended up being to John Kennedy Toole's vision without Belushi's *ever reading the novel*. Lily Tomlin, fresh off of *The Late Show*, is hilarious as Ignatius's mother. And that's a very young Frances McDormand as Myrna Minkoff. Sublime.

Malick's four-and-a-half-hour *Blood Meridian*, partially financed by star Marlon Brando (he sold off his island), is at once the best Western, historical and horror movie ever made. Brando underwent sumo wrestler training and had his head, eyebrows and body completely waxed to play the massive, hairless, indestructible Judge Holden. The Comanche attack sequence is both beautiful and nearly unwatchable. Watch Barry Brown carefully during the final confrontation scene in Fort Griffin. He had himself hypnotized. Despite the on-screen tension, Hackman and Brando were fast friends on set. The meteor showers that open and close the film were real.

∎∎∎∎∎∎∎

August 3 and 4

Stalingrad (1988)
dir: Sergio Leone

Opening with a close-up of the muzzle of a cannon and closing with a similar close-up of a crying newborn's mouth, Leone's *Stalingrad* is a blazing loop of war and rebirth. No one's ever been able to spot Clint Eastwood, Eli Wallach or Lee Van Cleef among the *half a million* background actors, but all three stars and the director insist they're there.

∎∎∎∎∎∎∎

PATTON OSWALT

August 5, 6 and 7

ORSON WELLES DOUBLE FEATURE!

Heart of Darkness (1942)

and

Batman: Riddle of the Ghoul (1944)

Welles starved himself down to a human skeleton to play Kurtz in *Heart of Darkness*. His jittery, no-sleep, diet-pills performance is worth the shadowy slog upriver with Joseph Cotten that makes up the first hour of *Heart of Darkness*. Welles steals the movie from the movie itself.

And who'd have guessed that Gary Cooper could pull off the roles of the Dark Knight Detective *and* Bruce Wayne? But somehow he slides perfectly into the tuxedo and the cowl, a tormented, urbane playboy who becomes a driven, taciturn bruiser by night. And leave it to Welles to populate his movie with *six* of Batman's cast of villains: Lee Marvin as Two-Face, Edward G. Robinson as the Penguin, Ella Raines as Catwoman, Dwight Frye as the Riddler, Everett Sloane as the Scarecrow and, towering imperiously over the whole mad feast, Welles himself as Ra's al Ghul. The Richard Widmark cameo, at the end, as the newly scarred Joker, leaping toward the screen from the smoking ruins of the chemical plant, still makes people scream. The costumes that longtime fans wear to midnight showings only add to the chiaroscuro carnival.

■ ■ ■ ■ ■ ■ ■

August 8 and 9

Weeping Blade, Laughing Bullet
dir: Seijun Suzuki
Whisper of Panic
dir: Allen Baron

Was there ever a loopier, more existential revenge plot than in Suzuki's lost yakuza drama, set among the go-go clubs and gambling halls of modern-day Tokyo? Jo Shishido is a disgraced yakuza hit man who decides he can regain his honor if he steals a samurai blade from a museum and uses it to kill his beloved prostitute girlfriend, who, he believes, is the last living descendant of a corrupt dynasty of shoguns. If I tried to explain to you how a razor necktie, Spirit's "I Got a Line on You" and an opium-addicted horse figure into the plot, your head would explode.

And then *Whisper of Panic*, Allen Baron's follow-up to his 1961 film *Blast of Silence*. Peter Falk (whom he originally wanted for *Blast*) is "Blind" Billy Farnum, a war veteran hotel detective with a piece of shrapnel from a Korean hand grenade embedded in his skull. He talks to it. There are voices from behind the door of one of the suites. A girl in trouble. He kicks in the door and realizes it was the shrapnel, fooling him into becoming a white knight. Except the room isn't empty. And it's the last person "Blind" Billy wants to see.

■ ■ ■ ■ ■ ■ ■

August 10 and 11

CAROLE LOMBARD DOUBLE FEATURE!

Ride a Cockhorse
and
Emma

A plane crash took "the Profane Angel" off the planet when she was thirty-three. Here, in the infinite, she's ageless and perfect. Perfectly insane in King Vidor's adaptation of Raymond Kennedy's *Ride a Cockhorse*, and perfectly charming (and dimwitted) in Michael Curtiz's *Emma*.

■ ■ ■ ■ ■ ■ ■

August 12 and 13

KENNETH ANGER DOUBLE FEATURE!

On the Road
and
The Ticket That Exploded
(both starring James Dean and Sal Mineo)

We can only show these with Kenneth in attendance. Luckily, he's one of the few living people allowed to cross over to this side, if only briefly. He's bringing mescal and fireworks. And yes, we've set up the eight projectors needed to show *The Ticket That Exploded*.

■ ■ ■ ■ ■ ■ ■

August 14

GRINDHOUSE DOUBLE FEATURE!

Space Jockey
dir: Phil Tucker (1952)
Billy Jack vs. Blacula
dir: Melvin Van Peebles and Tom Laughlin
(1977)

Phil Tucker directed *Robot Monster*, which jostled shoulders with *Plan Nine from Outer Space* and *The Beast of Yucca Flats* as the worst movie ever made. But Phil Tucker, in an interview for the book *The Golden Turkey Awards*, hinted darkly at another, "lost" film he made, called *Space Jockey*. And he asserted that it was ten times worse than *Robot Monster*.

Go watch *Robot Monster* sometime. Then think about the director of that film bragging that he's got something even worse. In the movie palace I'm building for you, Sherman, you're going to be the first to see it.

And, I mean, *Billy Jack vs. Blacula*. That should have happened long before I ever thought of it here. Tom

Laughlin barefoot-kicking the stake through the vampire pimp's heart in the opening scene still gets applause.

▪ ▪ ▪ ▪ ▪ ▪

August 15 and 16

Superman
dir: Sam Peckinpah
Doctor Strange
dir: Francis Ford Coppola

Yes, at one point Peckinpah was developing *Superman*, and Coppola briefly had the rights to Marvel Comics' *Doctor Strange*. I *want* these movies to exist. They won't. So here they are, in my head.

Steve McQueen is a revelation as the moody, determined, tragic Last Son of Krypton. Warren Oates is loathsome and magnetic as the Parasite. And fuck it, Gene Hackman is still Lex Luthor. Has to be. Ali MacGraw is miscast as Lois Lane, but if you wanted McQueen in the seventies . . .

Coppola's *Doctor Strange*. I mean, where do I start? Three hours. Gordon Willis cinematography. A young Christopher Walken, prowling the streets of early-seventies Greenwich Village, fighting demons and the establishment. The hidden Avengers "cameos" are also fun to spot.

▪ ▪ ▪ ▪ ▪ ▪

August 17 and 18

DISNEY DOUBLE FEATURE!

Half Magic
and
The Phantom Tollbooth

Classic, 2-D cel animation by the Nine Old Men. Edward Eager's book *Half Magic* was so truly enchanting that it was the one time Walt ever let the Nine Old Men have carte blanche. What they came up with was so unprecedented, so gorgeous (and such a blockbuster), that when it came time to do *The Phantom Tollbooth*, Walt reportedly said, "I'll see it when it premieres." Again, his instinct didn't fail him.

■ ■ ■ ■ ■ ■ ■

August 19, 20 and 21

JERRY LEWIS DOUBLE FEATURE!

The Day the Clown Cried
and
The Catcher in the Rye

I am proud and ashamed that the slang term "Oswalt's briefcase" has become shorthand for revealing any forbidden work to the public. Now that I'm older, I think what I did was wrong, that day in Jerry Lewis's office. But the briefcase is opened, and it's out there, and even though it isn't good, *The Day the Clown Cried* always fills a theater. And I'm a snatch-and-grab thief, forever.

But Lewis's true dream was to be Holden Caulfield, and watching the nervous, seventeen-year-old Lewis make his film debut (and subsequently pursue a dramatic acting career, only once venturing into comedy when he played opposite John Belushi in *Noble Rot*) is a wonder. Those eyes, those pain-filled eyes.

■ ■ ■ ■ ■ ■

August 22 and 23

MICHAEL REEVES DOUBLE FEATURE!

The Wasp Factory
and
The Land of Laughs

Michael Reeves. Twenty-five years old when he died. Barbiturate overdose. Four brilliant films and then gone. Here's where you get to see his intense, hilarious adaptation of Iain Banks's *The Wasp Factory* and his hilarious, intense, much-debated version of Jonathan Carroll's *The Land of Laughs*.

■ ■ ■ ■ ■ ■

August 24 and 25

RUSS MEYER DOUBLE FEATURE!

Jaws of Vixen
and
Mmmmmmmmounds!

What happens when the breast-obsessed director has a dump truck full of money? I'm not going to spoil either of these with a description. But you get to find out—*twice*. And that's Christy Hartburg—SuperLorna from *Supervixens*—as the Nude in the Tube. Testosterone bliss.

■■■■■■■

August 26, 27 and 28

HITCHCOCK DOUBLE FEATURE!

The Boy Who Followed Ripley
and
I Was Dora Suarez

Hitchcock at his most subtle (*Ripley*) and lurid (*Suarez*). Fascinating to watch back-to-back, since *I Was Dora Suarez* violates Hitchcock's principle of making an audience wait for a shock. In *The Boy Who Followed Ripley*, the shock only comes after the final, tortured fade-out, when you fully realize what has happened. And in *I Was Dora Suarez*, the opening scene is *all shock*. And then we slide into inexorable, slow-motion dread until that last graphic scene with the rowing machine and the final judgment of the Nameless Detective—superbly played by Michael Caine.

■ ■ ■ ■ ■ ■ ■

August 29 and 30

BUSTER KEATON DOUBLE FEATURE!

Hassle Magnet
and
Masters of Atlantis

Hassle Magnet was Keaton's glorious, roaring return to form after sobering up in the late sixties. It was also a sly love letter to the kung-fu films he secretly loved, hilariously taking the piss out of the concept of the "ballet of violence." And his stone-faced tour de force in *Masters of Atlantis* won him a much-deserved Oscar, which he shared with costar Art Carney.

■ ■ ■ ■ ■ ■ ■

SILVER SCREEN FIEND

August 31 and September 1

SCORSESE DOUBLE FEATURE!

The Hawkline Monster (1974)
(starring Robert De Niro and Harvey Keitel)
The Moviegoer (1978)
(starring John Cazale)

And now we're at the end of the month. Scorsese's poisoned love letter to the sixties, *The Hawkline Monster* is as darkly hilarious as *Raging Bull*, as well as an elegiac ode to the unrealized, childlike mysticism of the Summer of Love, turned sour and mirrored in De Niro and Keitel's hit-men duo Cameron and Greer (stand-ins for every Nixonian dirty trickster who smirked behind mirrored sunglasses and went unpunished).

And *The Moviegoer* is my thank-you to you, Sherman. Cazale's searching, knowing eyes, blinking from too much time staring at a flickering screen, finally realizing that what he's searching for lies in the real world and outside of his books and films. You asked me to hand you a script after four years. That question sent me back out into the sunshine. Let's see if I can bring back something to unspool in the dark.

The Second-to-Last Night Café

April 15, 2009

"We're going to hold her up. Don't look down."

That's the doctor in the delivery room. He's just cut my daughter out of my wife's womb. Amy Winehouse's "Rehab" is playing softly on the sound system. My wife is smiling, drugged and blissful, humming along.

The doctor holds up my daughter. She takes a big gulp of hospital air, her ribs flaring against her pink-and-purple skin from the effort, and lets loose a squalling blast that hits me harder than any Sergio Leone pistol shot, Donald Sutherland pod-person scream or Steve McQueen tire squeal.

I entered this eight-sided, all-white delivery room dressed like a helmetless astronaut. I'm going to emerge a dad. I'm going to see many fewer movies. I still might not ever get to make one. But I came close enough to being consumed by them to know how to raise a human who's drawn to the wide-angle world stronger than to any flickering movie temple.

We'll see.

There's one more Night Café after this one. But none of us return from that one.

We'll see.

Collected Writings
on Film

This is the first thing I wrote about film, for a never-published monthly newsletter that Tales Café planned to publish. It was written in the autumn of 1996, when I was on a serious *film noir* binge.

I Watch Crime Movies

Blinking neon . . . shot glasses . . . forty-cent breakfasts . . . bent cops . . . worried wives . . . desert roads . . . fog and overcoats . . . snitches . . . heavy ashtrays . . . office coffee . . . secrets . . . "shiners" . . . neckties . . . bundled money . . . honest criminals . . . interrogation rooms . . . hideouts . . . interstate fugitives . . . kids in jeopardy . . . too-loud jazz . . . dapper psychos . . . knowing bartenders . . . guns . . . fists . . . lipstick . . . street lamps . . . vengeance and failure . . .

I like any film about criminals working their work. Professionals, psychos, kingpins and snitches, those "in the life" and the unknowing citizens they're trying to screw. Every aspect, every angle—run *anything* on me. As long as it's about someone deciding to cross the line and then *trying to get away with it*, you've got my attention. Crime! Crime! Crime!

The best crime movies were made back in the forties and fifties. That's when everyone lived under the Big Honking Lie—that Security and Justice and Worth were given to people who worked hard and were honest. Sure, there were Bad Elements out there—burglars, rapists, dope fiends. But the Bad Elements were quickly and soundly brought down by the Law. And hardworking people who made the right decisions continued to live life untainted, unruffled and with a stress-free sleep schedule.

Anyone can point out the Big Honking Lie. Crime films show you the BHL *in action*—churning innocent and guilty alike into hamburger. You're in that meat grinder, too. Most films are an escape—crime films are a not-so-helpful assurance that hey, at least you're not alone in hell.

Crime films give you another reminder—that your wretched, insignificant life plays out like Epic Drama to you. *You're* the hero (wronged or rewarded) in the Saga of Your Life—and *everyone else* (minor players in Your Saga) is living under the same delusion. No wonder the cities are filled with motion, heat, hate and violence. That the wide-open countryside makes people heave axes through their loved ones' skulls. Perspectives are reversed, morals are stained and the few who can navigate the mirror-maze of America are left beaten, broke—stripped and screwed of everything but their integrity and wisdom. The crime films of the forties and fifties showed you this muddy swirl of right and wrong in crisp black and white.

Monster movies are reassuring. The beast will be defeated. The sun comes up. Most science fiction films are numbing. We're all lurching into the future with jet packs and lasers. Ten percent of all comedies are funny. The other 90 percent are pranks. Westerns are history. Romance films are science fiction.

And that's fine. Movies are supposed to distract and entertain. You're fooling yourself if you think otherwise. Big, loud, bright and bouncy. You can *get* that it's a fireworks show and go on with your own, full life. Or you can *not* "get it" and provide entertainment for those that *do*—as you try to make your life "like it is in the movies." Sucker!

That's why crime films are my favorites. They're the *one type* of film that assures us life sucks and will *continue* to suck after we leave the theater.

But they make the failure seem so stylish. So intoxicating.

So *epic*.

When AFI was putting out its "100" lists, I wrote this, mainly for myself, about my one hundred favorite movie moments. Completely personal, unapologetic and honest—these things stayed with me. One of those things that truly surprises you while you write it.

Uncle Bill recording his lines in *American Movie*

The night-swimming sequence in *Cat People* (1942)

Jean-Claude Van Damme, Dennis Rodman, Mickey Rourke *and* a tiger fighting in a minefield inside the Roman Colosseum at the end of *Double Team*

Spina Bifida Sister from *Pet Sematary*

The monsters getting their invitations during the opening credits of *Mad Monster Party*

The last eight minutes of *Blood Simple*

The first fourteen minutes of *Raising Arizona*

Frances McDormand's awkward "date" in *Fargo*

Jeff Bridges explaining the "newest shit" in the back of the limo in *The Big Lebowski*

Robert Redford's on-air crack-up in *The Candidate*

Albert Finney getting ready for bed in *Murder on the Orient Express*

Zander Schloss singing "Feelin' 7-Up" at the beginning
of *Repo Man*

Two great movie dads played by the same actor: Paul
Dooley in *Breaking Away* and *Sixteen Candles*

Peter Boyle negotiating his fee with George C. Scott in
Hardcore

Scene-stealing performance in a film no one saw: Oliver
Platt as "the Toad" in *Zig Zag* ("Gimme knobbyjob!")

Chevy Chase crying in the desert with Anthony Michael
Hall in *Vacation*

Great performance in a great film: Eric Bana in *Chopper*

Great performance in a good film: Jackie Gleason in
Smokey and the Bandit

Great performance in a shitty film: Dana Olsen as spoiled
rich asshole Palmer Woodrow in *Making the Grade*

The news reports in the original *Night of the Living
Dead*

Zombies prowling to the Muzak in the original *Dawn of
the Dead*

"Send more paramedics" from *Return of the Living
Dead*

Celebrity target practice in the *Dawn of the Dead*
remake

Blade's entrance at the blood rave

John Malkovich's insane, Wile E. Coyote death at the end of *Con Air*

The gunman eating the dead guy's candy bar in *Broken Arrow*

Alan Rickman in *Die Hard*

Bill Murray getting baptized in *Ed Wood*

The sad, ironic final twist in *Le Trou*

The funny, ironic final twist in *The Taking of Pelham One Two Three*

Joe Don Baker ordering breakfast at the whorehouse in *Charley Varrick*

Laird Cregar watching the film of the dead woman in *I Wake Up Screaming*

Ella Raines "seducing" Elisha Cook Jr. in *Phantom Lady*

The final "frames" of *Two-Lane Blacktop*

Gene Wilder's complete fucking meltdown ("I do . . . NOT . . . WANT . . . TO . . . LIVE!") in *Young Frankenstein*

Bullet deflected with a bullet in *Full Contact*

Marina Zudina outrunning the hall lights in *Mute Witness*

Columbo's first "appearance" in *Diabolique*

Don Cheadle's interrogation technique in *Devil in a Blue Dress*

"You've gotta be fucking KIDDING!" from John Carpenter's remake of *The Thing*

Bill Paxton's face when he overhears the two city cops making fun of him in *One False Move*

"We belong dead" at the end of *Bride of Frankenstein*

The senile child molester tracking the girl around the lake in *Never Take Sweets from a Stranger*

Peter Cushing's line "PACK! We're LEAVING!" in *Frankenstein Must Be Destroyed*

Hearing-aid torture in *The Big Combo*

The end credits sequence from *Wild Things*

Brad Pitt mumbling, "Fucking condescend to *me*," in *True Romance*

The reel of rescued kisses at the end of *Cinema Paradiso*

"Why don't dey just call him 'Girl George' and get rid of all dah CAHN-foo-shun?" from *Commando*

The scarred girl releasing the animals at the end of *Eyes Without a Face*

Allen Baron stalking through Harlem in *Blast of Silence*

Target practice in *The Day of the Jackal*

The Klumps at the all-you-can-eat buffet in *Nutty Professor II*

Nelson de la Rosa in *The Island of Dr. Moreau*

Peter Falk telling the story about the "eagle-sized" tsetse flies carrying off the brown babies during the dinner party in *The In-Laws*

Lukas Haas's speech on the White House steps at the end of *Mars Attacks!*

"*James Caan.* Is that real enough for you?" from *Real Life*

"Hulk running" in *Modern Romance*

Albert Brooks's crossing-guard job in *Lost in America*

The apocalyptic gunfight at the end of Takashi Miike's *Dead or Alive*

Ben Stiller in *Heavyweights*

Ed McMahon's disembodied, accusatory floating head emerging from the depths of space at the beginning of *Daughter of Horror*

Edie feeding the raccoons in *Grey Gardens*

Morgan Freeman asking Kathy Baker which eye she wants to keep in *Street Smart*

John Wayne shooting out the dead Comanche's eyes in *The Searchers*

The freeway battle in *The Matrix Reloaded*

The song "Up There" from *South Park: Bigger, Longer and Uncut*

Philip Baker Hall explaining the rate card in *Hard Eight*

Bachelor Party: "I just bet my balls, and shook on it."

Revenge of the Nerds: "I thought I was looking at my mother's old douche bag, but that's in Ohio."

Heathers: "Football season is over, Veronica. Kurt and Ram had nothing left to offer the school except date rapes and AIDS jokes."

Christy Hartburg dancing toward the pay phone in Russ Meyer's *Supervixens*

Joy Harmon washing the car in *Cool Hand Luke*

The screaming contest in *The Vanishing*

The fucking contest in *Sweet Sweetback's Baadasssss Song*

Alan Arkin introducing "Geraldine" in *Wait Until Dark*

Robert De Niro ambushing Sean Bean with coffee in *Ronin*

Pee-wee Herman dancing his way out of a biker beating in *Pee-wee's Big Adventure*

Unk pontificating on the tenement roof in *Hated*

Eli Wallach assembling his gun in *The Good, the Bad and the Ugly*

Leatherface's chainsaw death dance at the end of *The Texas Chainsaw Massacre*

Bill Pullman as "the stupidest person on the face of the earth," Earl Mott, in *Ruthless People*

The first ten minutes of *Final Destination 2*

John Candy's side of the phone conversation in *Uncle Buck*

Thelonious Monk spinning around and around in circles in *Straight, No Chaser*

Samuel L. Jackson's interrupted monologue in *Deep Blue Sea*

Jon Voight's winking corpse in *Anaconda*

Julie Christie explaining the brothel biz to Warren Beatty in *McCabe & Mrs. Miller*

TV MOVIE MOMENT #1: Scott Jacoby coming out of the woodwork in *Bad Ronald*

TV MOVIE MOMENT #2: John Cassavetes putting the beat-down on Ronald Reagan in Don Siegel's *The Killers*

Chris Holmes on the pool raft with the "vodka" in *The Decline of Western Civilization II: The Metal Years*

Andy Kaufman going on a killing rampage in *God Told Me To*

The abandoned pavilion in *Carnival of Souls*

Jeff Daniels and Lauren Holly's snowball fight in *Dumb and Dumber*

Ray Sharkey shadowing Peter Gallagher's onstage moves from the sidelines in *The Idolmaker*

The final, tidal-wave-of-blood samurai duel in *Sanjuro*

SILVER SCREEN FIEND

John Lennon battling the Glove in *Yellow Submarine*

Jack Black cradling the dead rabbits in *Jesus' Son*

Joe Pantoliano screaming, "Everybody's telling me to go
fuck myself!" in *Midnight Run*

These next five reviews were written for *Ain't It Cool News* back in the nineties, when I was writing under the name "Mr. Molly." That's Joe Don Baker's character in *Charley Varrick*, by the way.

"You're Cold Now"

Blast of Silence

Guess what, crime film junkies? Your *Carnival of Souls* was shown last night at the Egyptian here in Hollywood. That's right—Allen Baron's ultra-rare *Blast of Silence* had a screening last night, with the director/star/screenwriter in attendance, dishing his own flick!

Released in 1961 and made for $28,000, *Blast* rivals *Seven*, *Juggernaut* and *Get Carter* in the "Bleak"-stakes. The plot is so simple it may as well not even be there—a hit man returns to his old neighborhood in Harlem to complete a contract, but is waylaid by his own personal memories crashing in on him. The "blast" in the title refers to his own, self-wished death.

Schrader and Scorsese must have caught *Blast of Silence* at some time in their lives, because watching hit man "Baby Boy Frank Bono" prowl the night streets is like watching a rough draft of Travis Bickle. The voice-over narration (by an uncredited Lionel Stander, and not Baron—representing a colder, more idealized self-vision of Bono's) sounds like Travis forty years down the line.

The cinematography, by Merrill Brody, who also edited, is crisp, dark and menacing. Baron pointed out, pre-screening, that they had an early Arriflex, and no dolly (Brody had to weigh the tripod down with bags of sugar). The tracking shots, through Madison Square and Harlem, are terrific, even more so considering the resources.

There's a superlative review of *Blast* in RE/SEARCH's *Incredibly Strange Films*, which is where I first read about it back in 1991. A twelve-year wait for a seventy-seven-minute black-and-white crime film? Worth every minute. Baron himself said, after the screening, "I'd give it a ten for cinematography, and a two for story."

He's wrong. Tens all around, and a plea for someone to put this thing on DVD. What a blast.

—MR. MOLLY

The Anvil Chorus

Blue Collar

If you've ever worried that, lying on your deathbed, you'd utter, hopelessly, "My God, I never saw a shirtless dildo fight between Harvey Keitel and Richard Pryor," then put your fears to rest. Paul Schrader's *Blue Collar*—his directorial debut after writing obsessive masterpieces such as *The Yakuza*, *Rolling Thunder* and *Taxi Driver*—features just such a scene.

Said dildo fight happens during a sweaty, exhausting,

ultimately hopeless low-rent orgy scene, midway through the movie. Our three leads—Keitel, Pryor and Yaphet Kotto—play laborers on the Checker Cab assembly line in Detroit. Their lives are sweat, oil, fumes, flame and frustration. Every conversation on the line is a barked argument. Every union meeting is a chance to speak truth to powerlessness and smirking condescension. At night, they go home to unfilling meals of Hamburger Helper, intrusive IRS agents interrupting their numbing hours in front of silly-ass shit-coms and drinking themselves into dry oblivion.

It's pointless to repeat the whole "Major studio movies in the early seventies would be little indie films nowadays" mantra. But *Blue Collar* is a refreshing exception—this probably wouldn't even get made as an indie today.

Remember when art direction and costume design were as thoughtful and creative as the screenplay and direction? In *The Taking of Pelham One Two Three*, Walter Matthau dressed in the drab, slouchy sort of suit a transit cop would be able to afford. *Melvin and Howard*'s world of trailers, junk food, coupons and jury-rigged appliances are as much characters in the film as the actors. And was there ever a more alive, breathing, growing/dying Western town than in *McCabe & Mrs. Miller*?

The characters in *Blue Collar* wear give-away T-shirts from McDonald's and outfits made of the same, repurposed six or seven clothing items. Their "break room" is an alcove full of rusted snack dispensers that belch out stale candy bars and oversweetened instant coffee—when they don't flat-out steal your money.

And the "chemistry" between the three leads is, at

best, tense. This is the kind of "friendship" that develops between the desperate and pressured—wobbly, and abandoned at the first sign of selfish hope. The fact that *any* sort of give-and-take exists between Pryor, Keitel and Kotto on-screen is a miracle because, according to Schrader in the DVD commentary, the three actors hated each other. Fistfights, arguments and threats were the norm for any working day. The laughter between the three—on the line, in the bar after work and, later, as they plan a heist—is only there to cool the flames of hatred and violence.

Yes, they plan—and execute—a heist. Pryor—here playing a work-shirking, fast-talking con man—notices the safe in the union headquarters is under-guarded and usually left open. Desperate for money (at one point he "borrows" the neighbor's kids to try to fool an IRS inspector into believing that he actually has all the kids he claims on his taxes) he convinces Keitel and Kotto to go in on the job. Both of his friends are in similar financial straits—unsolvable, self-inflicted financial holes they'll never dig themselves out of.

But what they find in the safe is more valuable than money, and ultimately, their doom. Not to spoil any of the surprises in the second half of the movie, but *Blue Collar* goes places with its story and characters that even a gritty independent might be uncomfortable visiting.

So many things to love about this film. The soundtrack, especially the unnerving, machine-driven score, with Captain Beefheart growling over an anvil chorus ("Dark meat by the pound / Hard work *fucking* man"). The documentary shots of the assembly lines, like the industrial ballets of *Metropolis* and *Brazil*, but robbed of all grace and poetry. The way goofy comedy mixes so seamlessly with anger and violence in scene after scene. Yaphet Kotto, an avenging angel against the union's eerie thugs, who ultimately pays a grisly price for his strength and intelligence. Keitel, complaining of "brain cancer" and kids' braces, reduced to an automaton by the film's end, whose only humanity left to him is whatever violence he can inflict. Lane Smith and Ed Begley Jr. and Leonard Gaines and the great Harry Bellaver as the ineffectual union president.

And Richard Pryor. If you only know him from *The Toy* and *Superman III*, then watching *Blue Collar* will be a refreshing shock. Still as profane, true, mean and funny as he ever was onstage, Pryor here is also scary, sad and all-too-human as Zeke, the biggest fly in the company ointment. If the company can't crush a noisome fly, it can do something far worse. You'll see.

Keep those cabs rolling out. Never stop the anvil chorus. Grease the gears.

Those Checker Cabs. Was that a conscious choice on Schrader's part? The fact that these cabs, the same model Travis Bickle piloted in *Taxi Driver*, came from a hot, hopeless hell like the factory in *Blue Collar*? Where every rivet was fastened by someone with murder on his mind? Every windshield tamped into place by someone who wanted to blow up the world? Every steering column and gas pedal affixed by the damned? It's as if the metal, rubber and fuel themselves were infused with rage. Bickle never stood a chance.

—MR. MOLLY

My Flick-Nerve Is Flat

An (Ultimately) Disappointing
Evening with Jan Kounen

Wednesday, September 20, was VIBROBOY: AN EVE-
NING WITH JAN KOUNEN IN PERSON at the Egyptian Theatre on Hollywood Boulevard. The American
Cinematheque, which screens flicks at this boss vintage
theater, had shown his short LE DERNIER CHAPERON
ROUGE (THE LAST RED RIDING HOOD) a few
months ago. The response, according to their mailer, was
overwhelming. Thus, the entire evening.

Let me start by saying Jan Kounen is probably the clos-
est we'll ever get to a live-action Tex Avery. That is, if
Avery had Russ Meyer's libido and David Lynch's revul-
sion/love of the human body and all of its functions. Jesus
Christ! Blood arcs through the air. Pores sweat rivers. Eyeballs bulge and jaws flex like they contain steam pistons.
Every angle is spastic, every pull-in a crash-zoom. Even a
CONVERSATION between two people, standing outside
at a clothesline, is cut like a Sergio Leone gunfight. And
all in French! *Sacre bleu!*

Kounen doesn't like you taking yer eyes off of the
screen. EVER.

At seven p.m. they screened three shorts. GISELE
KEROZENE (1990), which I realized I'd actually seen years
ago in San Francisco. Five minutes long, fucking brilliant.
Post-punk drag queen witches zoom around a deserted
office park (Kounen likes deserted office parks, it turns

out) on sputtering, gas-powered brooms. "We dare you to count the edits and camera set-ups," boasted the program. Well, there's a bunch of 'em, plus a genius "cameo" by a certain DC superhero, in his "mild-mannered" disguise.

VIBROBOY (1994) followed, and was the weakest of the bunch. It also portended things to come. An abusive white-trash couple and the drag queen they love to hate run afoul of an ancient Incan (?) idol, which contains "Vibroboy," which seems to be the malevolent spirit of angry, throbbing cocks. Yeah, I was confused, too. Twenty-eight minutes of some pretty intense spousal abuse, homophobia and an extended offscreen ass-rape set to a lovely rendition of "Parle moi d'amour." Has to be seen to be dis-believed.

Then came THE LAST RED RIDING HOOD. Wow! Coproduced with Caro (of CITY OF LOST CHILDREN Jeunet and Caro), who plays the part of "the Monster," this is a graphic/lovely children's horror-musical about a banished monster, an atomic rocket containing "100 Little Red Riding Hoods," and a heroic/villainous Big Bad Wolf. There are these unbroken, herky/swooping extended shots (especially during the musical numbers—YES, MUSICAL NUMBERS!) which had me slavering in anticipation for DOBERMANN, the full-length feature they were screening at nine.

Kounen spoke in between films. About his commercial and video work (I can't help thinking he did that Lamb video I see pop up on 120 MINUTES to disturb my sleep every now and then), about how VIBROBOY was his desire to see "stupid assholes given superpowers," about the DVD of his complete short films, videos and commercials—encoded ONLY for European DVD players! Rat-shit!

Then came DOBERMANN, which I think was based on a French comic book. I was sitting with David Goyer, who said at one point they were considering Kounen for BLADE 2, after watching a ten-minute screener of DOBERMANN. *Considering* being the key word.

DOBERMANN is SO over the top it comes BACK around to blast its way up your ass. The opening sequence alone—a baptism that ends with a gurgling baby fingering its first gift, a .357 Magnum—is like MANON OF THE SPRING compared to the rest of the film. I remember Pauline Kael describing STAR WARS as being like a "box of Cracker Jack that is all prizes." DOBERMANN is a crime/action film that's all exit wounds.

Keep in mind, there are some sequences that literally lift you from your seat. A shoot-out in a rave club where EVERYONE involved, cops and criminals alike, is on PCP. Shot through their POVs, including the POV of Dobermann's deaf lover, it's like watching John Woo trying to prove his manhood by sheer body count and muzzle volume.

Come to think of it, Kounen also enjoys his drag queens.

And that's the lead-up to the CLIMAX. The CLIMAX! Until that point we've seen grenades stuffed into motorcyclists' helmets, families tortured, flaming bodies blown through the air to be snuffed in the Seine and a criminal wipe his ass with CAHIERS DU CINEMA. There are twice as many bullets coming at you as lines of dialogue. Characters are defined by how and why they bleed and die. Dicks are blown off. Faces are literally scraped off on the pavement. To give you an idea of who you're forced to root for (at moral gunpoint), Dobermann's nemesis is a cop so brutal he enjoys watching a woman be nearly kicked to death by her boyfriend in the street, and thinks nothing of tossing a man's baby through the air (and later dropping a grenade into its crib) to get information. He does, however, suffer one of the funniest (and cleverest) "double-deaths" I've seen in a long time. If MAXIM magazine ever does a flick, Kounen's hired.

It was just TOO GODDAMN MUCH, in the end. Even THE ROAD WARRIOR, THE MATRIX and DIE HARD had lulls. Catch your breath, wait for the next "topper." I love Milky Way bars, but I don't want eight of them for dinner.

—MR. MOLLY

Writing Porn with Blood and Feathers

Quills

I got to see Philip Kaufman's newest, *Quills*, at the William Fox Theater.

Let me say first off I'm a sucker for those "writin' with feathers" flicks some old-time Hollywood studio head said he hated (might have been Warner, but don't quote me). Loved *Dangerous Liaisons*, *Ridicule*—if they're writing with feathers and plowing each other under eight skirts, I'm in.

So I figured Kaufman, with his love of visual texture,

would serve up a veritable Sizzler buffet of powdered-wig porking and poking.

Quills is exactly that, with rich performances and brilliant art design. Everyone acts like they're tanked on ether, and can't wait to get in front of the camera and try out that new accent they bought on eBay.

The plot concerns the twilight years of the Marquis de Sade (Geoffrey Rush, doing a Casanova Frankenstein with good dialogue), when he was locked in a French asylum, whiling away his time staging plays with inmate talent, and writing his most famous works, smuggling them out with the help of a maid (Kate Winslet, who gets yummier and yummier despite what the skeleton-worshipping fruits over at *Us* magazine say).

Wait a minute, I've got my laptop set on "run-on sentence." There.

The Marquis has another ally in the asylum's warden/priest (Joaquin Phoenix, his big eyes simultaneously pleading with God and his own libido) who's convinced the Marquis is exorcising his inner demons through his writing. Of course, the popularity of lash-and-bum tomes like *Justine* brings the attentions of a Puritan doctor (Michael Caine) who is determined to "break" the Marquis and strike a blow for fuddy-duddies everywhere.

I could go into the loopy plot, over-the-top performances (Rush, in particular, has been to the Harvey Keitel School of Art House Acting) and ironic ending, but none of that's going to do the job of GETTING YOU TO SEE THIS MOVIE, which you should. Because it's more fun than a box of bonbons shaped like tits.

The Marquis, locked in his cell, is a priapic Hannibal Lecter, whose pen and tongue turn everyone around him into heaving fuck-beasts. There's a Feast of Fools sequence in which the Marquis taunts Caine's character, who's recently taken a child bride. There's a brilliant sequence in which the asylum's maniacs must transport de Sade's latest work, sentence by sentence, to a waiting Winslet, like an X-rated game of Telephone (a scene which inspires the film's best line of dialogue, spoken by Rush, and not revealed here). And, pen and paper denied him, de Sade goes to some . . . ahem . . . brutal lengths to get his writing read.

Have a dinner of squab, and a bottle of Yquem, and instruct your coach driver to get you hence to the nearest picto-graph theater. Get a nice box over the orchestra, crack a package of Venus's Nipples and support perversion.

It's the Christmas season, after all.

—MR. MOLLY

The Eyelid-Droop, the Mop and the Rictus

Timothy Carey, *The World's Greatest Sinner*
If you have any sense, you'll go to the Egyptian Theatre on Hollywood Boulevard on Saturday, November 4th, and Sunday the 5th. If you DON'T have any sense, you'll probably be there already.

For two nights the American Cinematheque is screening Timothy Carey's ultra-rare THE WORLD'S GREATEST SINNER (1962). I first caught this flick back in January of 1996, when it got screened once at the New

Beverly Cinema. Someone told me it was John Cassavetes's favorite film. Maybe they meant "favorite comedy," since this is one of the strangest moviegoing experiences I've ever had. I felt like the be-wigged gentry, paying a few shillings to view the lunatics in Bedlam back in the eighteenth century.

The film concerns Clarence Hilliard (Carey), an insurance salesman who decides he's "God" (he makes a shirt with the word *GOD* stitched onto the sleeves) and forms a rock band/religion/political movement. It reportedly took Carey FOUR years of off-and-on piecemeal filming to complete the project. The closing credits alone are a testament to this, and worth the price of admission. You'll see what I mean, guaranteed. Never has the idea of written/directed/starring/edited/filmed been more lovingly illustrated.

The plot could politely be called "episodic," unraveling like a vaguely sinister acid trip, only you're laughing too hard to start clawing your eyeballs out. The soundtrack is by Frank Zappa (billed in the credits as "ZAPPA") and it churns along like a forgotten garage rock band recorded in an echo-ey sewer—and that's a compliment! The scenes of Hilliard performing in "concert" make the Shaggs look like Rush. The band basically bangs and crashes and farts out this proto-punk spew, then stops dead silent so Hilliard can yawp, "Please, please, PLEASE take my HAND!" Then the band starts up again, with Hilliard doing this creepy/hilarious shimmy dance, jangling around in his weird silk blouse/shirt.

Of course, these moments pale in comparison to the

scene where he seduces a seventy-year-old widow for her cash, and the final, climactic "miracle." Trust me, you HAVE to go see this flick.

It's also nice to see the burgeoning DVD "bonus goodies" mentality starting to infect live screenings. Saturday night's screening (six p.m.) is introduced by Romeo Carey, who's showing a thirty-minute work-in-progress documentary about his father. Then, at nine, they're showing THE KILLING (1956) and THE OUTFIT (1973).

Sunday's screening (seven forty-five p.m.) is followed by TWEET'S LADIES OF PASADENA (1970), Timothy Carey's attempt at a late-night TV series. Rumor has it he turned down a part in THE GODFATHER so he could finish TWEET'S—a one-hour show about the only male member of a Pasadena sewing circle (Carey) who find clothes for nude animals. TWEET'S is followed by CINEMA JUSTICE, a six-minute outtake from Steve DeJarnatt's TARZANA, where Carey sustains an unscripted rant as a crazed Korean War vet. I've never seen either one, but you can bet your death-rictus I'll be there! Whew!

—MR. MOLLY

From my website, this is "The Johnny Lawrence Story," my half-assed attempt to do a David Thomson *Suspects* piece. William Zabka himself read it and liked it. Kiiiiiya!

"Sweep the Leg and Wake the Gimp"

The Johnny Lawrence Story

Johnny Lawrence owned the universe in 1984. The universe was, to him, the wealthier part of the San Fernando Valley (and not that shithole Reseda) but it was his first and, he hoped, last horizon. High school was a nonstop carnival of Cobra Kai karate classes, make-out sessions with Ali (his hottie girlfriend) and doled-out skull-bashings to any spindly nerd crossing his swaggering path.

But his universe flickered senior year. First, Ali dumped him. Then, a skinny, olive-skinned New Jersey asshole named Daniel LaRusso appeared. Worse, it looked like he and Ali were flirting, hooking up . . . *right in front of him*!

He and his Cobra Kai buddies tuned up LaRusso as best they could. At first on the beach, and then in a nighttime knuckle session outside the high school's Halloween dance. Johnny had been smoking some righteous ging, and for a second felt like he might actually be able to kill Daniel. Hadn't his Cobra Kai instructor always said, "An enemy deserves no mercy?" There were times, when he was deeply stoned, that Johnny wished he *were* a cobra.

All sleek, and smooth, and leathery. Beyond speech and remorse, and kept in a crate.

And hadn't his father always admonished: "I will move you so far the fuck away from this town if I *ever* see you back down from someone smaller than you"? The old man, with his gray hair, bulgy eyes and potbelly, holding sway over a car wash empire that had made him a multi-millionaire. Johnny loved, feared and hated him.

So Johnny fed his father an elaborate lie about being jumped by eight Mexicans when he and his crew were stopped mid-thrash by LaRusso's only friend—a pudgy, sawed-off Asian maintenance man.

But that maintenance man was the last thing to go wrong for Johnny that year. He took LaRusso out to a junkyard and imparted some kind of ancient Chinese ass-kicking secret to the goddamn shrimp, and in the end it only took a single Crane Kick to shatter Johnny's San Fernando Universe.

His father, sickened and mortified, immediately moved Johnny to a new school, forcing him to finish his senior year under the name of "Greg Tolan." He also forbade Johnny to practice any martial arts. Heartbroken, but paralyzed with fear of his father, "Greg" took to mind-lessly hoisting cafeteria tables, taking a perverse thrill in seeing people and food spilled onto the ground.

What was this new, sexual charge he felt? He was a bad boy making a big messy-poo, and seeing things splash and make a stainy-wainy made him want to be punished, pad-dled, humiliated. He didn't like thinking too deeply about it. But he was happy.

For a while. Because sure enough, another skinny, olive-skinned boy hove into view. He even looked like Daniel LaRusso (even though he dressed like Elvis Costello). This new kid seemed more . . . delicate. Feminine. What were these *feelings*?

It was too much for "Greg." At a beach dance (another fight on another beach), he threw the Daniel LaRusso look-alike into the ocean. But his satisfaction was short-lived. The new kid's wigger friend knocked "Greg" unconscious with a single punch.

Back home, Johnny's father was apoplectic. His summer before college was a confused series of non-starts. He dated the bulimic girl next door before dumping her from a safe distance when she took a family trip to Europe. Then Johnny's father packed him off to college, where he went under the name "Chas." The smell of the sea haunted him, and he quickly took up diving as a sport. Splashing into the water, over and over again. Diving headfirst into oblivion, like he'd always wanted to.

But goddamnit, here was yet another olive-skinned, dark-haired little wimp in his life. Was his life ever to be free of gawky shrimps? This one didn't even give Johnny the courtesy of beating the shit out of him. He simply took his girlfriend away, like it was the third act of some badly written comedy, where the writers simply needed the little shrimp to hook up with the impossibly hot older girl. It made no goddamn sense. And then, as if the gods had become tired of pissing on him and had decided to start shitting, the shrimp's gray-haired father (the spitting image of Johnny's own dad) defeated him in the diving finals, doing a ridiculous dive called the "Triple Lindy." It was as if his own father had finally, publicly, rejected his spawn, painting Johnny's defeat in the sky in a series of midair somersaults.

Johnny dropped out of college and drifted to Los Angeles. He wandered into a pawnshop to see if there was an old karate *gi* he could buy. The burly man behind the counter told him he might have something in the basement. Johnny followed him, not even hearing the whistle of air as the leather sap crashed against his skull and his world turned black.

They cut out his tongue and dressed him in zippered leather, making him look like a mutant cobra. They sodomized the memory of every olive-skinned, dark-haired shrimp from his mind forever, and for that he was grateful. The store owner and his mascara'd security guard friend, light years away from his distinguished, hated father, became his new family.

When they woke him up to watch over their newest prey—a bald, intense boxer who they left tied up while they "partied" with his gangster buddy—he was no longer "Johnny Lawrence" or "Greg Tolan" or even "Chas." He was "the Gimp." His life consisted of his box, the protein shakes they fed him through a straw, blaring fifties rock 'n' roll and his monthly Handi-Wipe bath. That's why he started screaming, tongue-less, when the bald boxer worked himself out of his straps and made his escape. And when the boxer sent a crashing right hand into the Gimp's melon, Johnny's last thought was a sincere thank-you to the laughing gods that at least it wasn't a goddamn Crane Kick.

This is a short story I wrote for a website called
Popcorn Fiction (now MulhollandBooks.com), which
was based on an outline for a vampire movie idea I had.
Foodie vampires.

Tasting Menu

Amuse bouche

The town car pulled into the circular driveway off Lookout Mountain Drive. A lesbian couple owned the house. They had adopted two plump, sweet-blooded Chinese babies the year before.

The Driver emerged. In his black suit, *à la page* shirt and custom loafers, he looked like a living slice of the car's inky mass, peeling itself from the chassis, moving on its own. He opened the left rear passenger door.

"Appetizer course?" murmured the Girl as she squinted in the bright moonlight. The Driver smiled, his dead eyes masking his usual mix of contempt, despair and amusement when dealing with his passengers.

He took in her boots, low-cut jeans and faded concert T-shirt, her little-girl ponytails and $3,000 clutch handbag. Her maroon, lipsticked mouth was an infected bullet hole in her pale doll face.

Before the Driver could walk over to the opposite passenger door, the Boyfriend stepped out.

Jesu Cristo, the Driver thought. He'd picked up the couple at their stylish downtown work/loft half an hour ago. They weren't used to chartered livery service; the Boyfriend had clattered into the car before the Driver could open the door for him, not even scooching over for the Girl.

And now here the Boyfriend stood, lit by the moonlight like a cheap plastic figurine in an aquarium. Sunken cheeks, cow eyes trying to be "haunting," black leather blazer over a black T-shirt with black jeans and black goddamned everything. There were times when the Driver, musing, thought how unnerving it would be to see a vampire dressed in an Easter-y polo shirt and khaki slacks. But these pups didn't have the presence or confidence to be startling or original. Not them, nor any of the others in their vast litter. Maybe the next one. The Driver had centuries—behind him, and yet to come.

In his head, he replayed the last moments of magic hour in Wisconsin in 1936, the girl's screams, the *phut*-THWACK of the thresher, her father not twenty feet away, thinking his un-weddable daughter had finally found a man who'd love her, the sweet corn-silk of her hair and blood, an American vintage no longer made. The Driver could smell the sweating cast iron of the thresher's frame mixed with the raw corn perfume when the Boyfriend's voice snapped him back to the dull present.

"*Nice*," said the Boyfriend. He held the baby by its punctured fontanel. The Girl sprawled on the couch, piddling her fingers in the torn-open neck of the lean, buzz-cut lesbian, who'd begged for her daughter's life.

The Driver blinked, confused. He'd blocked out the whole, dull entry to the house. He'd daydreamed through the tedious screams and alarms. And he'd managed to ignore, awake, the grinding sameness of the feed.

"I find the pearly rice and steppe-grass undertones of Asian infants to be a wonderful palate awakener," said the Driver, remembering his glorious autumn in Nanjing.

"Yeah, babies fuckin' *rip*," said the Girl.

Sweet and sour

The Driver made the sloping right onto Sunset from Laurel Canyon. Behind him, the Boyfriend and the Girl polished their sticky maws with the mint-scented wipes the Driver always provided. The wipes flowered gracefully from a glazed Buddha. He wondered if either of them would get the visual reference.

No. The Girl tongue-washed her incisors while the Boyfriend dug in his jacket pocket for something. *Here it comes*, thought the Driver.

"Could you play this mix CD while we drive?"

The Driver smiled with his mouth and not with his eyes and said, "I'd be happy to."

He slid the disc into the car's player, praying, *Not Bowie Not Bowie Not Bowie Not Bowie Not Bowie Not Bowie*.

The opening piano figure from "Lady Stardust" filled the car.

He tried to pay better attention as they entered the nightclub but his infinite, sprawling mind wandered. He could barely focus, even as the Girl and the Boyfriend double-sucked the big, rangy blonde in the private, sound-proof suite overlooking the dance floor. Her husband—stocky, soft and content where she was ropey, sharp and demanding—sprawled over the little coffee table, his neck snapped, purple blood pooling under the skin from a burst throat artery. Paralyzed, he was aware but helpless. He watched his trophy wife sucked to a husk. The Driver sipped a weak, Finnish vodka and thought of Rome.

"This is . . . this is *fantastic*," gasped the Girl between swallows. "Like her blood is fighting its way out of my belly."

"The ambitious always give one a solid flush," said the Driver.

"Uh, oh *man* . . . ," started the Boyfriend, searching for a cliché.

The Driver continued, cutting him off. "Take a sip of the male. The dominant in a couple is a perfect counter-point to a milky dependent. Sharp and savory, then sweet."

The Boyfriend nodded. Like all dilettantes, they took his words as gospel. It was the dismissive, professorial tone, the Driver had learned. Flattened the gullible without fail.

Conversation

"Los Angeles."

The Girl said, "The City of Angels."

Godfuck, here come the City of Angels musings, thought the Driver. The blood was on them, he reminded himself, and the inanity would get worse before it got better. And, he chided, it would not get better.

"Do the angels know the devil prowls their streets tonight?" mused the Boyfriend, aloud and unashamed.

"Two devils. Two devils hunting angels," said the Girl.

The Driver rolled his eyes as Mazzy *fucking* Star played. Devils were for dimwits. And angels were for Oprah.

A deep red

They headed east on Fountain, settling into the driveway of a big, brick house in Hancock Park. An old screenwriter lived there. His movies were regarded by cineastes and rep theater ghouls as complex, layered classics that yielded up new and startling insights into humanity, love, loss and joy with each viewing. He'd been unemployable since the early eighties, steadily writing newer, richer works every two years, all of which piled up in his cluttered garage. A recent appreciation in *The New Yorker* asserted that one of several wealthy indie tyros should sack up and film one of these scripts.

The Girl tore out the old man's throat in his office. The Boyfriend sloppily drank from the blue femoral artery, visible under the papery, pale skin. The screenwriter writhed but stayed pinned to the floor. The Driver read the last full page the man would ever produce. He wrote on an Olympia manual typewriter.

The scene took place between a man and a girl he'd dated in high school. From only three exchanges of dialogue, the Driver was able to perceive everything about the two people—the man's empty success, his need to impress the only girl he'd ever really loved and her heartbreaking confusion at his need, and her genuine concern for him that would never again ripen into love. It was elliptical, funny and sad. The Driver couldn't think of a single current actor or actress who could pull it off.

He looked over at the gobsmacked Girl, almost crosseyed with the depths she'd just ingested. The screenwriter carried rich oceans of pain, beauty and memory inside of him—all of it wasted, he was sure, on the couple who'd hired him for the evening's feast.

"Juicy," gurgled the Boyfriend. "Was Bruce Willis in any of this dude's movies?"

Roast garlic and a palate cleanser

Twenty minutes later the Driver found himself thinking of Sicily again, and of Afdera's eyes when they lit the oiled *fagots* under her. It was a memory he thought he'd stored away, but the olfactory senses had a hidden punch.

The Girl and Boyfriend were ten yards away from him, licking the last drops from the two Armenian Power gangbangers they'd goaded down the alley behind Zankou Chicken. *It's the garlic*, thought the Driver. *The goddamned garlic smell is taking me back to Sicily.*

The Driver reminded himself to gently discourage the

garlic course to his clients in the future. He did not want to think of Afdera again. He cut his tongue on the tip of his left incisor, a trick he used to chase away unwanted memories, or combat boredom.

The Girl and Boyfriend were worrying every last drop from the Armenians. It was the only way they could safely ingest garlic, and the fact that it was deadly any other way made it a treat true as black truffles. The couple had paid extra to guarantee its place on the evening's menu, and the Driver, above all else, was a professional.

As a palate cleanser, the Driver fed them a trust-fund hipster at an overdecorated condo in Silver Lake. His blood was thin and weak, but had an earthy, clean undertone from all the espresso. Too much of a coward to do heroin, and too unimaginative to ever fuck anyone truly dangerous, he was free of narcotics and disease. The couple each took healthy mouthfuls, and then let his tattooed carcass shudder to the floor. The Driver thumbed through the usual, morose collection of Bukowskis, Portises and . . . wait . . . there it was. *A Confederacy of Dunces.*

Always.

(Always! Always! *Always!*)

Dream meals

On the long drive north on the 5, to the 134 and deeper into the Valley, the Girl and Boyfriend had this conversation:

The Boyfriend: "Well, Andy Warhol. That'd have been my dream feed."

The Girl: "For real? He'd be pretty thin stew, you ask me."

The Boyfriend: "That's what I think he projected, you know. Put *out* there. But I bet that façade hid *depths*."

The Driver remembered a dismal night at the Factory in 1964. He was instantly repelled by Warhol—a mumbling neuter who gorged on cheap Whitman's chocolates and emitted soupy waves of Chanel No. 5 to cover the stench of not bathing. Then again, the *Warhola* pack had always been coffin-worms. The only amusement of the evening was when Andy tried putting the Driver in one of his insipid films. It was a childish experiment. Warhol thought he might be able to capture the Driver's reflection in the tinfoil glued to the walls.

The Girl: "Yeah, maybe."

The Boyfriend: "Well, we already know *yours*, don't we?"

The Girl: "Fuck yeah, you do. Three films and out? I mean, the scene in the whorehouse, with his mother? For that scene *alone*, I bet he'd be great to drink. And when he says, 'You're tearing me a-*paaaaaart!*' "

The Boyfriend: "The knife fight at the observatory's my favorite."

The Driver shuddered. A hydrophobic, self-loathing homosexual—*that* was her dream feed?

Fish & pasta

"This is where we're going for the main course? The *Valley?*"

The Boyfriend said, "Yeah. Why aren't we going into Beverly Hills?"

Because Beverly Hills is nothing but thin, gruel-y Jews. Or briny Iranians basted in rage and religious terror, thought the Driver. *Not that either of you'd know the difference. And what* is *the difference, considering what waits for you when we reach the ocean?*

"When you see what I've prepared, you'll forget all about Beverly Hills," chuckled the Driver.

This was the one course he wished he could have sampled, but it went against the rules of cuisine. The Driver stood at the entrance of the living room. The walls rippled with the light of the outdoor pool. Soon the light was gone as blood spread on the pool's surface. A cloak on a candle.

The Girl was shaking the last mouthfuls from the wife, whom the Boyfriend had chased earlier out to the diving board while the Girl killed the husband. They'd each drunk half—per the Driver's instructions—and then switched wineskins.

Now the Boyfriend quietly took the last, polite mouthful from the husband before reverently lowering the body to the carpeting.

The dead man had been an amazing TV sketch comedian. Funny and bright and ironic, the clownish covering of a mind darker than the sluice channel in an abattoir. The pain and neglect he'd inflicted on the wife, over the years—the years of affairs and subsequent, halfhearted reconciliations—had given her the earthy undertone of a poet's graveyard. His guilt, half-acknowledged and half-denied and diluted from his psyche through ever more desperate, eager-to-please public performances, gave his blood a metallic, otherworldly tang. Liar's fuel.

It was a perfect pairing. The Girl and the Boyfriend were sated and dizzy.

Cognac and coffee

You can feel the sea before you see or smell it, even when you've been dead-alive as long as the Driver. The Girl and Boyfriend, not as long removed from the salty womb of life, bounced up and down on the backseat.

"Lesskill a surfah!" slurred the Boyfriend, blood-drunk from the evening's meal. The Girl giggled, and nodded her head like a sandpiper dipping for sea crabs.

"You both . . . deserve a dessert to match the richness of your tastes," stated the Driver. It was the first compliment he'd paid them all evening, and it quieted them like petting a dog.

The Driver produced a bottle of No. 7 Collection *Erté* Courvoisier as they walked up the winding driveway to the cliff house. The deadly ocean roared against the rocks below them.

The Boyfriend said, "Should I pay you now? What's your tip usually like?"

"My tip is always left to your discretion."

"Well . . . uh, well. You were really cool and all, I appreciate it. We're gonna do this again with some friends," said the Boyfriend, fumbling a leather billfold from his pocket and producing a thin stack of hundreds. The Driver noted the three dots of blood on the top note, but said nothing. "And, uh, keep the change. I mean, there's a lot in there for the, uh, the tip."

The Driver took, folded and pocketed the bills with a fencer's grace and swiftness. "I look forward to another evening."

"Yeah, it was great," said the Girl. "And we'll make another mix tape. Have you ever heard Cibo Matto?"

The Driver opened the door to the house and gestured for them to enter. They both smiled nervously and went inside.

"Is that . . . ?" The Boyfriend stood, halfway between shock and a lunge. The Girl, still dizzy, crouched, but it looked more like a curtsey.

The dessert course sat at the end of a long granite table in the minimalist dining room. An almost-empty bottle of ouzo, with maybe three fingers' full of the clear liquid at the bottom of the bottle, sat in front of him. His doughy, bloated face showed the effects of years of starchy food and sweet alcohol. A half-eaten loaf of bread and a pottery urn of oil were at arm's length.

"The infamous Hunter of . . . our kind has been through a slow decline these last few years," said the Driver, as if describing a cave-aged cheese.

"*This* is where he disappeared to after slicing Brontis? To fucking *Malibu*?" spat the Girl.

"As you can see, the stress of—" But the Girl and Boyfriend didn't wait for the Driver to finish his presentation. He didn't think they would.

The Hunter hadn't, either. The night before, he'd said, "They won't be able to restrain themselves. Not with the way she felt about Brontis. And not with how badly her new coyote pup boyfriend wants to impress her. They'll be on me before they realize there's no alcohol smell coming off me."

He was right. They knocked him backward from his chair, the Girl taking the throat and the Boyfriend demurring, taking the femoral like the bottom dog he was.

One mouthful was all they got. They leaped off the Hunter as if shocked. He struggled to his feet, opening a drawer in the low sideboard and taking out gauze, tape and antibacterial spray. He didn't even bother looking as the Girl and Boyfriend swelled and blackened like overripe peaches in the sun, going all waxy and billowy and suddenly bleeding out, collapsing in a wave of blood and bruised flesh. The gore swirled in a pool around the wide drain in the subtly concave concrete floor of the anteroom, where two Bacons and a Klee were displayed. A thin plastic hose, coiled in a covered recess in the wall, would later spray away the last traces of their demise. The Driver noted that the wall spatter had missed *Head VI* by inches. *How* many times had it missed?

The Hunter was bandaged and bound and cleaned and he sat back at the table. He drank the last swallow of water from the ouzo bottle, making an exaggerated, "Ahhhhhhh!"

"It is fortunate all the wine you pour into yourself doesn't dilute that holy water," said the Driver, trying to look distracted. Behind his back, his fingers clawed like spiders, anticipating.

"Nothing dilutes a rageful blessing," said the Hunter. "Apparently."

From a different drawer in the sideboard he produced a small velvet bag. The top was secured with string. He tossed it to the Driver, not even looking when he did so. A small smile fluttered at the side of his mouth as he heard the Driver gasp.

The Driver worried the bag open and there, in the loamy Sicilian soil, was a burnt finger bone. He tried to remember the warm flesh that once covered it, the flesh he'd tickled secretly as they sat in vespers.

"Bit by bit. And I give you a Hunter's oath you'll finally have of her 'that which can bring her back,' " drawled the Hunter.

"The trophies I've delivered haven't proven my intent? You can't give me her heart and trust we'll part as professionals?" asked the Driver, his voice trembling. And then, "This isn't vampiric enough, what you're doing?"

The Hunter uncorked the pottery urn of Sicilian olive oil and watched the Driver's face. When he saw what the oil's smell did to his memory, saw the painful ghost of Afdera flicker across the Driver's face, he smiled.

And he said, as he poured a mournful pool of oil onto a plate, and tore an end of bread, "She wasn't always yours. And I want"—he bit into the soaked crust—"to make a meal of it."

"I'll wait / In the pouring sun"
Frank Black
"Los Angeles"

*Finally, this introductory essay for The Dissolve
the day it launched.*

12 Tour Guides

This website is going to cover movies. I can't think of a better collection of writers to guide you, constant visitor, through what's turning out to be both a cataclysm and rebirth of what it means to conceive, execute, distribute, view and ultimately talk about—and argue about—cinema.

With that in mind, why not look at a dozen of my favorite "tour guides"—not only in movies, but in books, songs and comics?

There are a few iconic characters I left off this roll call—and I'm willing to hear counterarguments. The three ghosts in Dickens's *A Christmas Carol*, the Scarecrow in *The Wizard of Oz*, the Emcee in Fosse's *Cabaret* and, finally, Beetlejuice (who rises from his crypt wearing a "Guide" cap)—all of them don't make the list. Dickens's ghosts are each focused on showing Scrooge one specific event or object—if anything, they're QVC presenters. The Scarecrow is just as surprised as Dorothy by the people and situations they encounter on the way to Oz, and is essentially a traveling companion. The Emcee, despite being demonic enough to rise above the petty politics of both the Kit Kat Club *and* the Third Reich, is a snarky, singing commenter, and doesn't see the pink triangle and striped pajamas in his future. And Beetlejuice isn't interested in guiding anyone anywhere.

Unlike . . .

The poet Virgil in Dante's *Inferno*. One of the first, still one of the best. Who better to guide you through hell than a Roman poet?

Actually, I can think of a *lot* of better people, but Virgil does a slick job leading midlife-crisis-suffering Dante through the first part of his *Divine Comedy*. Dante's hell is a barely coded laundry list of personal grievances and score settling, inflated to the level of eternal damnation. I can't blame him—ten minutes in line at Trader Joe's and I'm imagining every satanic torment within the cosmos on the people in front of me.

One line from canto XXI has always haunted me, however. While crossing a little bridge, Dante alludes to a discussion he and Virgil have of which his "Comedy does not dare tell." Wait, *what*? Considering the tsunami of rape, torture, forced shit-eating, disembowelment and extreme awfulness that follows, what in the fuck could they have been chatting about that would make Dante think, *My readers are* not *going to want to hear this*?

Where are the DVD extras on classic literature?

Speaking of "classic literature," I would now like to include guides from two graphic novels. If you listen carefully, the moment I put the words "classic literature" and "graphic novel" in the same sentence, Harold Bloom's head exploded.

But Sir William Withey Gull in Volume Two of Alan

Moore's *From Hell* and the Trenchcoat Brigade in Neil Gaiman's *The Books of Magic* are the evil and good, dark and light opposites of each other, as far as guides go. Especially guides of the supernatural.

Despite all of the gaslit gore, coal-black killing and Victorian disembowelments in *From Hell*, the most chilling scene comes early on, before a single murder: Sir William's carriage ride through London. Netley, the illiterate coachman, is our confused, increasingly alarmed stand-in for Gull's rapid-fire monologue about the history hidden in London's streets, its link to male magic and the sinister design which traps the city's inhabitants inside a gigantic, ever-unfolding "magickal" rite. It's Iain Sinclair channeled through a far scarier "mad doctor" than Frankenstein, Moreau or Lecter, told to an idiot who realizes too late the maze he's trapped in. Eddie Campbell's pen-and-ink crosshatching, like hasty morgue sketches, only deepens the darkness.

Then there's Neil Gaiman's Trenchcoat Brigade—four of DC Comics' most enduring magical heroes (including Alan Moore creation John Constantine), guiding a young boy, Timothy Hunter, through DC Comics' occult universe. Dubbed "the Trenchcoat Brigade" by Constantine (to the annoyance of the other three—the Phantom Stranger, Dr. Occult and Mr. E), the four issues of *The Books of Magic* are an amazing stand-alone story by themselves (and act as a more adult prequel to the Harry Potter novels) but also a good-hearted reminder that sometimes even tour guides are in as much danger— and are as lost—as those they guide.

We're about to make the jump from books to movies, but we get there by way of song. A friend of mine from the UK once told me, "Of *course* the film industry was centered in California. The light's so even and perfect out here." Later on, when I became a regular guest on Steve Jones's delightful *Jonesy's Jukebox* on the now-Internet-only Indie 103.1, he wondered aloud how any Briton could disparage Los Angeles. "Why would you trade the weather out here for the gray and rain of London?"

Yep. Brits love California, especially Los Angeles, and specifically, within Los Angeles, Hollywood. And in "Celluloid Heroes," Ray Davies takes you on a mopey tour of the Hollywood Walk of Fame, making lewd jokes about Rudolph Valentino, clumsy jokes about Bela Lugosi and poignant, gorgeous statements about Marilyn Monroe and Bette Davis. But he gives the most positive accounting to, who else, another Brit—George Sanders, who "if you covered him in garbage" would "still have style." Pretty accurate, since George ended his movie career in the distinctively trashy movie *Psychomania*, before killing himself and leaving a suicide note that said, elegantly, "I am bored."

The idea of the musical tour guide, naturally, made its way to videos. Fee Waybill, in the Tubes' "She's a Beauty," led a bumper-car-ride pre-pube teen through censored nipple posters and stark, early-eighties New Wave girls in cages. Holly Johnson, the lead singer of Frankie Goes to Hollywood, popped up in a music-video-inside-a-feature-film in Brian De Palma's *Body Double*, leading a befuddled Craig Wasson through what had to be the most expensive porn shoot in history. If pornos normally have Béla Tarr–length handheld shots and Busby Berkeley-level choreography, then I'm watching the wrong pornos.

But it's ol' Diamond David Lee Roth (or, in the words of Andy Prieboy, "Good King David Lee Roth"), in the video for his cover of the Beach Boys' "California Girls," who remains the king of the music video tour guides. Splayed on a conveyor belt like a fresh tuna roll, pointing out your eighties MTV masturbation fodder, wearing a white vest and fedora—David Lee Roth was seemingly as confused about and ravenous for sex as us teenagers. Sex was fucked up when I was a teen. It was fucked up when *everyone* was a teen, and always will be. But we won't always have a Diamond Dave to dance us through the jungle.

There's nowhere to go beyond David Lee Roth in terms of music videos, so we might as well talk about movies. And we'll start small and subtly, before ascending to where most of you can guess we're going.

Like "Joey" in Philip Kaufman's *The Wanderers*. The jittery, David Byrne–in–his–teens character, as played by John Friedrich, while clearly a stand-in for author Richard Price's adolescent self, also serves as a brief guide to all of the different ethnic gangs who make up the sixties-era North Bronx. In a terrific, chaotic sequence near the beginning of the film, the diminutive Joey escorts Perry, his hulking, just-arrived protector, through the teeming hallways of their high school. That's where he points out the Del Bombers, Mau Maus, Pharaohs, Executioners, Wongs and, during a nightmarish later scene, the *28 Days Later*–like Ducky Boys. It's like a Marvel fan boy pointing out the various heroes, villains and random factions between them, all in a breathless patter.

House of 1,000 Corpses, Rob Zombie's directorial debut, has its fans and detractors, but does anyone *not* love Sid Haig's cackling, having-a-ball performance as Captain Spaudling, the proprietor of the "Museum of Monsters and Madmen," the forgotten granddaddy of every early-nineties hipster/ephemera/memorabilia store? His spiel during the low-rent, charming and creepy "murder ride" is a foreshadowing of the meat grinder our four annoying protagonists are about to be dropped into. If only they knew how to listen un-ironically . . .

There is nothing ironic about either "the Narrator" or "the European" in Alexander Sokurov's *Russian Ark*, a POV tour through Russia's endless Hermitage Museum. Transported back in time depending on what masterpiece they're standing in front of, both of the guides in this film are fearful of attacks from the figures they're showing us. As severe and gloomy as a Russian winter, *Russian Ark* is a guided tour through Mother Russia's wary, weary soul.

New York's soul is wary and weary, too, but it disguises its spiritual exhaustion under a cheap mask of aggression and impatience. Which is why there's no one better wired to lead us through it than Timothy "Speed" Levitch, in Bennett Miller's superlative documentary *The Cruise*. I saw it in theaters three times. Couldn't get enough of Levitch's living-Internet brain, zipping through Greenwich Village on the roof of a Gray Line tour bus, pinging every literary, artistic, musical and cinema connection that gets within ten blocks of his roving eye.

I remember, post-9/11, the Academy Awards did a tribute montage of New York. All the usual shots and dialogue samples. But there was one they didn't use. I know *why* they didn't use it, but it's one of the most affirmative, hopeful and hilarious assessments of what Manhattan was, is and will be into the future.

It's a shot with Timothy in mid-profile, shot from his right side. His tour bus is passing through midtown Manhattan, and he says this, while gazing out of the rear window:

"You are sitting amongst the twentieth-century invention. A city that grew up at an explosion, as an explosion, that is an explosion; an experiment, a system of test tubes gurgling, boiling, out of control. Of radioactive atoms swirling. Civilization has never looked like this before. This is ludicrousness and this cannot last."

He then cuts his mike. There's a period to his paragraph in the form of a raspy *chhhh* as the mike cuts out. He spins, counterclockwise to his left, and, after considering the city, which he now views moving toward him rather than disappearing behind him, says:

"The new Ann Taylor store on the right."

It's going to be okay. Thank you, Timothy.

Which brings us to Wonka. Not the bearded tatterdemalion from the original illustrations in Roald Dahl's *Charlie and the Chocolate Factory*. And not Johnny Depp's Anna Wintour–dressed–as–Michael Jackson–for–Purim interpretation in Tim Burton's movie.

Nope. Gene Wilder. They may as well change the character's name to Willy Wilder at this point, he so owns the role.

There's been so much written about Wilder's interpretation—the fact that you can't entirely trust him, his weird, sadomasochistic undercurrents and the sly, passive-aggressive way he handles questions from the parents of the kids he's guiding through his chocolate factory. I remember, in the TV column of Seattle's *The Stranger* free weekly, a description of the show read, simply, "Children fight for survival in Willy Wonka's chamber of horrors." Not an inaccurate description.

So how about this, and I'll leave you in the able hands of *The Dissolve*'s staff. Willy Wonka, for all of his terrorizing, and cheating, and mockery and riddles, ultimately wanted everyone who visited his factory, and who tasted his wares, to *dream* better. To *imagine* better. And to take in the creative arts with the same level of originality as those who made it. The people who create—the singers of songs, the dreamers of the dreams—demand the same from the people they're trying to reach with their creativity. And I hope the same thing for the writers here at *The Dissolve*, as well as any future readers. Through passion, and arguments, and controversy and ultimately understanding, maybe you can pilot your way through the psychedelic tunnel that movies seem to be racing through now. And come out the other side with your imagination and perceptions stronger. Imagination is the only Everlasting Gobstopper we've got.

Acknowledgments

I've been very lucky in my life in terms of people who are able to tolerate me. How I've ended up amid the group of creative, infuriating, hilarious, truly beautiful people I call friends and family is beyond my understanding and outside of logic.

My wife, Michelle McNamara—thank you for being a companion, a sly mom, a safe home, and for being a much better writer than I can dream of being. I aspire to your level of expertise with the English language. So far I've made it a fourth of the way there. That failure makes me a highly competent writer.

Alice, who is five years old as I write this—I hope there are still movie theaters in your future. If not, I'll try to create the experience for you, or at least pass along the excitement and wonder.

My parents—Mom, for letting me watch the original *King Kong* on TV when I was three, and who had to explain to me that it wasn't a book where I could turn the page away from the scary/fun parts; Dad, for Sunday afternoons watching *The Great Escape* and *The Longest Yard* and *The Taking of Pelham 123*, which is what dads were supposed to do in the seventies.

My brother, Matt, a sprocket-fiend-come-lately and vengefully. Someone's going to let you point a camera at those writhing, fantastic screenplays you churn out. A mad billionaire, a wealthy cougar—I don't care. I just want to see them.

Michael Torgan and Julia Marchese, still manning the furnace and patching the hull of the New Beverly. Thank you for sharing your memories of Sherman and making sure there are memories to come in the future.

Everyone I used to see movies with at the New Beverly—Ben Schwartz; Karen Kilgariff; Drew McQueeney; David Goyer; Harlan Ellison; Josh Olsen; Joe Wagner; my brother, Matt (*Once Upon A Time in the West* on mushrooms!); Tim Kirk; Edgar Wright; Brian Posehn; Gerry Duggan; and Blaine Capatch. Thanks for the arguments, shared disbelief and joy and shared boxes of Red Vines.

My agent, Daniel Greenburg, for wrestling this second memoir from me; Brant Rumble, for having the patience with all of my blown deadlines; and Aja Pollock, for copyediting it into coherence.

Michael Weldon and Danny Peary and everyone at *The Onion A.V. Club* and *The Dissolve*.

And, finally, to the freaks—the ones who make the films and the ones who devour them. I don't know if I'll ever become the former, but it won't be for lack of being the latter.

CUT.

Four Years of Films

■ **1995**

Saturday, May 20, 1995
Sunset Boulevard and *Ace in
 the Hole*
New Beverly Cinema

Tuesday, May 23, 1995
The Nutty Professor
New Beverly Cinema

Sunday, May 28, 1995
Muriel's Wedding
Balboa Theater, San Francisco

Friday, June 2, 1995
Crimson Tide
Town Center 5, Encino

Saturday, June 3, 1995
Amateur
Sunset 5

Sunday, June 4, 1995
Die Hard with a Vengeance
Sherman Oaks Galleria

Wednesday, June 7, 1995
Touch of Evil
New Beverly Cinema

Thursday, June 8, 1995
Kiss of Death
New Beverly Cinema

Tuesday, June 13, 1995
Buster Keaton Shorts and
 Steamboat Bill, Jr.
New Beverly Cinema

Thursday, June 15, 1995
Little Odessa
Town Center 5, Encino

Saturday, June 17, 1995
Batman Forever
Sherman Oaks 2

Sunday, June 18, 1995
Bloodsucking Freaks
 (midnight show)
Sunset 5

Wednesday, June 21, 1995
Repulsion and *Knife in the
 Water*
New Beverly Cinema

FOUR YEARS OF FILMS

Saturday, July 1, 1995
Apollo 13
Sherman Oaks 2

Tuesday, July 4, 1995
The Road Warrior
New Beverly Cinema

Friday, July 7, 1995
First Knight
Sherman Oaks Galleria

Sunday, July 9, 1995
A Clockwork Orange
  (midnight show)
Sunset 5
Judge Dredd
Sherman Oaks Galleria

Saturday, July 22, 1995
The New Legend of Shaolin
Roxie Theater, San Francisco

Sunday, July 23, 1995
Last Tango in Paris
Red Vic Movie House, San
  Francisco

Friday, August 4, 1995
Dr. Strangelove
New Beverly Cinema

Sunday, August 6, 1995
La Jetée
New Beverly Cinema

Wednesday, August 9, 1995
The Bicycle Thief
New Beverly Cinema

Thursday, August 17, 1995
Hiroshima Mon Amour
New Beverly Cinema

Saturday, August 19, 1995
Belle de Jour
Los Feliz 3

Sunday, August 20, 1995
Peking Opera Blues
New Beverly Cinema

Friday, August 25, 1995
Kids
Sunset 5

Saturday, August 26, 1995
Desperado
Cinerama Dome (midnight
  show)

Tuesday, August 29, 1995
The 5,000 Fingers of Dr. T.
New Beverly Cinema

Wednesday, August 30, 1995
Blow Out and *Dressed to Kill*
New Beverly Cinema

Friday, September 1, 1995
The Usual Suspects
Los Feliz 3

Sunday, September 3, 1995
The Chinese Feast
Red Vic Movie House, San
  Francisco

Saturday, September 9, 1995
The Maltese Falcon
New Beverly Cinema

Sunday, September 10, 1995
Two-Lane Blacktop and *Cisco Pike*
New Beverly Cinema

Thursday, September 14, 1995
Unzipped
Los Feliz 3

Friday, September 15, 1995
Young Frankenstein
New Beverly Cinema

Sunday, September 17, 1995
Full Contact
New Beverly Cinema

Tuesday, September 19, 1995
The Deadly Cure
New Beverly Cinema

Friday, September 22, 1995
Funny Bones and *The Entertainer*
New Beverly Cinema

Saturday, September 23, 1995
Seven
Sherman Oaks Galleria

Sunday, September 24, 1995
Chinatown and *Klute*
New Beverly Cinema

Monday, September 25, 1995
Mute Witness
Sunset 5

Thursday, October 5, 1995
The Seven Samurai
Monica 4-Plex

Friday, October 6, 1995
Devil in a Blue Dress
Cinerama Dome

Saturday, October 7, 1995
Bride of Frankenstein
Alex Theatre

Tuesday, October 10, 1995
Abby
Nuart

Friday, October 13, 1995
The Abominable Snowman of the Himalayas, Stolen Face and *The Curse of Frankenstein*
DGA Theater (American Cinematheque)

Saturday, October 14, 1995
The Hound of the Baskervilles, Horror of Dracula, The Stranglers of Bombay and *These Are the Damned*
DGA Theater (American Cinematheque)

Sunday, October 15, 1995
*Never Take Sweets from a
    Stranger* and *Scream of Fear*
DGA Theater (American
    Cinematheque)

Wednesday, October 18, 1995
The Addiction
Sunset 5

Saturday, October 21, 1995
*The Revenge of Frankenstein,
    Die! Die! My Darling,
    The Mummy, Prehistoric
    Women, The Vampire
    Lovers, The Reptile* and
    The Plague of the Zombies
DGA Theater (American
    Cinematheque)

Sunday, October 22, 1995
*X: The Unknown, When
    Dinosaurs Ruled the Earth,
    Five Million Miles to
    Earth, Frankenstein Must
    Be Destroyed* and *Captain
    Kronos: Vampire Hunter*
DGA Theater (American
    Cinematheque)

Friday, October 27, 1995
Frankenstein (1931) and
    Dracula (1931)
Orpheum Theatre

Saturday, October 28, 1995
Leaving Las Vegas
Beverly Connection Cinema
High Sierra
New Beverly Cinema

Sunday, October 29, 1995
Get Shorty
Galaxy Cinema

Friday, November 3, 1995
Casablanca and *The Big Sleep*
New Beverly Cinema

Saturday, November 11, 1995
Copycat
Beverly Connection Cinema

Thursday, November 16, 1995
2001: A Space Odyssey
Cinerama Dome

Saturday, November 18, 1995
The Doom Generation
Los Feliz 3

Sunday, November 19, 1995
Solaris
New Beverly Cinema

Friday, November 24, 1995
Casino
Crossroads UA Cinema,
    Monterey

Tuesday, November 28, 1995
Carrington
Sunset 5

Friday, December 8, 1995
Il Postino
New Beverly Cinema

Saturday, December 9, 1995
Cinema Paradiso
New Beverly Cinema

Sunday, December 10, 1995
Grease
New Beverly Cinema

Sunday, December 17, 1995
Sherlock Jr. and *Pandora's Box*
Castro Theatre, San Francisco

Sunday, December 24, 1995
Rosemary's Baby (midnight)
Sunset 5
The Wizard of Oz and *Willy Wonka and the Chocolate Factory*
New Beverly Cinema

Monday, December 25, 1995
Nixon
Los Feliz 3
Georgia
Sunset 5

Tuesday, December 26, 1995
The City of Lost Children
Nuart
Four Rooms
Sunset 5

Wednesday, December 27, 1995
Babe
Fairfax Theater

Thursday, December 28, 1995
Toy Story
AMC 14
Citizen Kane
New Beverly Cinema

Friday, December 29, 1995
Twelve Monkeys
AMC 14
Sabrina and *Breakfast at Tiffany's*
New Beverly Cinema

Saturday, December 30, 1995
I Am Cuba
Sunset 5
Richard III
Beverly Center Cinemas

Sunday, December 31, 1995
Theremin
Sunset 5
The Killing and *The Asphalt Jungle*
New Beverly Cinema

■ **1996**

Thursday, January 4, 1996
Rashomon
New Beverly Cinema

Sunday, January 7, 1996
The Thing (1982)
New Beverly Cinema

Friday, January 12, 1996
Blue Velvet
New Beverly Cinema

Saturday, January 13, 1996
The Big Combo
Tales Café

Sunday, January 14, 1996
*The Horror Chamber of
    Doctor Faustus*
Red Vic Movie House, San
    Francisco

Saturday, January 27, 1996
Laura
New Beverly Cinema

Monday, January 29, 1996
Rififi
Tales Café

Wednesday, January 31, 1996
The World's Greatest Sinner
New Beverly Cinema

Saturday, February 3, 1996
Annie Hall and *Manhattan*
New Beverly Cinema

Sunday, February 4, 1996
The Shining and *The Exorcist*
New Beverly Cinema

Wednesday, February 7, 1996
The Seventh Seal
New Beverly Cinema

Thursday, February 8, 1996
Wild Strawberries
New Beverly Cinema

Saturday, February 10, 1996
The Big Heat
Tales Café

Friday, February 16, 1996
The Wild One
Tales Café

Sunday, February 18, 1996
Five Against the House
Nuart

Monday, February 19, 1996
Taxi Driver
Nuart

Friday, February 23, 1996
The Beat Generation
Tales Café

Saturday, February 24, 1996
If . . .
New Beverly Cinema

Thursday, February 29, 1996
Beyond a Reasonable Doubt
Tales Café
While the City Sleeps
New Beverly Cinema

Friday, March 1, 1996
Harold and Maude
New Beverly Cinema

Sunday, March 3, 1996
The Girl Can't Help It and
*Beyond the Valley of the
Dolls*
New Beverly Cinema
Girls Town
Tales Café

Sunday, March 10, 1996
Beware, My Lovely
Tales Café

Monday, March 18, 1996
The Window
Tales Café

Thursday, March 21, 1996
Mildred Pierce
New Beverly Cinema

Wednesday, March 27, 1996
Murder by Contract
New Beverly Cinema

Saturday, April 6, 1996
Naked City and *Undercover
Man*
USC
Up in Smoke
Vine Theatre

Sunday, April 7, 1996
Kiss Me Deadly
UCLA Melnitz

Saturday, April 13, 1996
Amarcord
New Beverly Cinema

Sunday, April 14, 1996
Yojimbo and *Sanjuro*
New Beverly Cinema

Monday, April 15, 1996
My Name Is Julia Ross
Tales Café

Monday, April 22, 1996
The Force of Evil
Castro Theatre, San Francisco

Wednesday, April 24, 1996
Berserk and *Strait Jacket*
New Beverly Cinema

Monday, April 29, 1996
While the City Sleeps
New Beverly Cinema

Tuesday, April 30, 1996
Vertigo
UCLA Melnitz

Saturday, May 4, 1996
Jail Bait
Nuart
Jaws and *Psycho*
Four Star Theatre

Sunday, May 5, 1996
Double Indemnity
Monica 4-Plex
Peeping Tom
UCLA Melnitz

Friday, May 10, 1996
Bob le Flambeur
Raleigh Studios, Chaplin
   Theater

Sunday, May 12, 1996
Obsession
Four Star Theatre

Wednesday, May 15, 1996
Pink Flamingos and *Female
   Trouble*
New Beverly Cinema

Sunday, May 19, 1996
Murder, My Sweet
Monica 4-Plex

Monday, May 20, 1996
Ruthless
Tales Café

Wednesday, May 22, 1996
Rebel Without a Cause
Four Star Theatre

Saturday, May 25, 1996
Pitfall
Tales Café

Sunday, May 26, 1996
Point Blank
New Beverly Cinema

Monday, June 10, 1996
Who Killed Teddy Bear?
The Castro Theatre, San
   Francisco

Tuesday, June 11, 1996
THX-1138
New Beverly Cinema

Friday, June 14, 1996
Switchblade Sisters
Sunset 5

Sunday, June 16, 1996
The Body Snatcher
Four Star Theatre (midnight
   show)

Saturday, June 22, 1996
La Cage aux Folles
Four Star Theatre

Sunday, June 23, 1996
I Was a Teenage Werewolf
Four Star Theatre (midnight
   show)
Diner
New Beverly Cinema

Monday, June 24, 1996
Caught
Tales Café

Wednesday, June 26, 1996
Singin' in the Rain
State Theatre

Saturday, June 29, 1996
The Last Waltz
Four Star Theatre (midnight
   show)

Monday, July 1, 1996
The Fallen Idol
Tales Café

Tuesday, July 2, 1996
The Search for One-Eye
   Jimmy
Music Hall

Wednesday, July 3, 1996
Independence Day
Golden State Theater,
   Monterey

Thursday, July 4, 1996
To Catch a Thief
Films in the Forest, Monterey

Friday, July 5, 1996
Phenomenon
Lighthouse Theater

Sunday, July 7, 1996
Gilda
Tales Café

Monday, July 8, 1996
The Crossing Guard
New Beverly Cinema

Tuesday, July 9, 1996
The Birdcage
Fairfax Theatre

Wednesday, July 10, 1996
The Tenant
New Beverly Cinema

Thursday, July 11, 1996
The Great Escape
Four Star Theatre

Saturday, July 13, 1996
It Came from Outer Space
   and *Earth vs. the Flying*
   Saucers
Nuart
Atlantic City
New Beverly Cinema

Sunday, July 14, 1996
Cool Hand Luke and *Hud*
New Beverly Cinema

Monday, July 15, 1996
Nightfall
Tales Café

Saturday, July 20, 1996
The Mysterians and *Village of*
   the Damned
Nuart
The Big Sleep (unreleased
   1945 version)
UCLA Melnitz

Sunday, July 21, 1996
Battle in Outer Space, *20*
   Million Miles to Earth and
   Shotgun Freeway
Nuart

Monday, July 22, 1996
Trainspotting
Showcase

247

FOUR YEARS OF FILMS

Tuesday, July 23, 1996
Once a Thief
New Beverly Cinema

Wednesday, July 24, 1996
Fled
Mann's Chinese Theatre

Friday, July 26, 1996
Supercop
Monica 4-Plex

Saturday, July 27, 1996
Scandal Sheet
Tales Café
*James Ellroy: Demon Dog of
    American Crime Fiction*
    and *Daddy-O*
Raleigh Studios, Chaplin
    Theater

Sunday, July 28, 1996
War of the Worlds
New Beverly Cinema

Wednesday, July 31, 1996
Multiplicity
Cinerama Dome

Saturday, August 3, 1996
Black Sunday
Raleigh Studios, Chaplin
    Theater
Lolita
New Beverly Cinema
The Party
Tales Café

Sunday, August 4, 1996
Evil Eye
Raleigh Studios, Chaplin
    Theater (midnight show)
The Nutty Professor and
    Kingpin
Sherman Oaks Galleria

Thursday, August 8, 1996
The Harder They Fall
New Beverly Cinema

Saturday, August 10, 1996
Cornered
Tales Café
Escape from L.A.
Mann's Chinese Theatre

Sunday, August 11, 1996
Picnic
Nuart

Tuesday, August 13, 1996
Thief
New Beverly Cinema

Thursday, August 15, 1996
Barbarella
Nuart

Saturday, August 17, 1996
Planet of the Vampires
Raleigh Studios, Chaplin
    Theater
Bad
New Beverly Cinema

Sunday, August 18, 1996
The Manchurian Candidate
Four Star Theatre
The Burglar
Tales Café

Monday, August 19, 1996
Kansas City
Sunset 5

Tuesday, August 20, 1996
Bonnie and Clyde and
    Badlands
New Beverly Cinema

Thursday, August 22, 1996
Suspiria
New Beverly Cinema

Saturday, August 24, 1996
*Hercules in the Haunted
    World*
Raleigh Studios, Chaplin
    Theater (midnight show)
Queen of Outer Space
Nuart

Sunday, August 25, 1996
The Island of Dr. Moreau
Mann's Chinese Theatre

Tuesday, August 27, 1996
*The Adventures of Buckaroo
    Banzai Across the 8th
    Dimension* and *A Boy and
    His Dog*
New Beverly Cinema

Thursday, August 28, 1996
Soylent Green and *The
    Omega Man*
Vine Theatre

Monday, September 2, 1996
California Split
Monica 4-Plex
Out of the Past
Tales Café

Friday, September 6, 1996
The Hippie Revolution
Nuart

Sunday, September 8, 1996
The Big Clock
Tales Café

**Wednesday, September 11,
    1996**
Pushover
New Beverly Cinema

Saturday, September 14, 1996
Maximum Risk
Mann's Chinese Theatre
The Palm Beach Story
New Beverly Cinema

Sunday, September 15, 1996
Marty and *The Apartment*
Four Star Theatre
The Blue Dahlia
Tales Café

FOUR YEARS OF FILMS

Thursday, September 19, 1996
Purple Noon and *The
    American Friend*
New Beverly Cinema

Saturday, September 21, 1996
They Won't Believe Me
Tales Café

Sunday, September 22, 1996
Assault on Precinct 13 and
    Escape from New York
New Beverly Cinema

Friday, September 27, 1996
Crossfire
Tales Café

Monday, September 30, 1996
All About Eve
Four Star Theatre

Tuesday, October 1, 1996
Planet of the Apes
New Beverly Cinema

Thursday, October 3, 1996
The Racket
Tales Café
Detective Story
New Beverly Cinema

Friday, October 11, 1996
The Man from Planet X and
    Night of the Living Dead
Orpheum Theatre

Saturday, October 12, 1996
The Cincinnati Kid and *The
    Thomas Crown Affair*
Four Star Theatre

Sunday, October 13, 1996
*Close Encounters of the Third
    Kind*
New Beverly Cinema

Monday, October 14, 1996
Napoleon
Four Star Theatre

Tuesday, October 15, 1996
Raiders of the Lost Ark
New Beverly Cinema

Wednesday, October 16, 1996
Bound
Mann's Chinese Theatre

Saturday, October 19, 1996
Phantom Lady
Tales Café

Tuesday, October 22, 1996
Beauty and the Beast
New Beverly Cinema

Thursday, October 24, 1996
Private Hell 36
Tales Café

Saturday, October 26, 1996
Gone with the Wind
Four Star Theatre

Thursday, October 31, 1996
Alien and *Aliens*
Four Star Theatre

Friday, November 1, 1996
Walk on the Wild Side
Tales Café

Saturday, November 2, 1996
Key Largo
New Beverly Cinema
Yojimbo and *A Fistful of Dollars*
Raleigh Studios, Chaplin Theater

Wednesday, November 6, 1996
The Lady from Shanghai
New Beverly Cinema

Friday, November 8, 1996
Blindman and *For a Few Dollars More*
Raleigh Studios, Chaplin Theater

Sunday, November 10, 1996
Criss Cross
Tales Café

Thursday, November 14, 1996
The Next Big Thing
Harmony Gold Preview House

Friday, November 15, 1996
Garden of the Finzi-Continis and *Swingers*
Town Center 5, Encino

Saturday, November 16, 1996
Space Jam
Mann's Chinese Theatre
Once Upon a Time in the West
Raleigh Studios, Chaplin Theater

Sunday, November 17, 1996
Secrets and Lies
Sunset 5
The Loved One
New Beverly Cinema
Ransom
Cinerama Dome

Saturday, November 23, 1996
Strangers on a Train (UK Version)
Nuart

Tuesday, November 26, 1996
Larger Than Life
Towncenter 3

Wednesday, November 27, 1996
Last Man Standing
Herndon Twin
Star Trek: First Contact
Reston Town Center

Sunday, December 1, 1996
The Rocky Horror Picture Show
Nuart (midnight show)
Drunken Master
New Beverly Cinema

251

Thursday, December 5, 1996
Sling Blade
Sunset 5

Friday, December 6, 1996
She Freak
Nuart

Saturday, December 7, 1996
The English Patient
Vista Theatre
All Through the Night
Raleigh Studios, Chaplin
 Theater

Saturday, December 14, 1996
Mars Attacks!
Mann's Chinese Theatre

Sunday, December 15, 1996
Daylight
Beverly Center Cinemas
Deadline at Dawn
Tales Café

Thursday, December 19, 1996
Dirty Harry
Castro Theatre, San Francisco

Friday, December 20, 1996
*Beavis and Butt Head Do
 America*
Royal Theatre, San Francisco

Saturday, December 21, 1996
Bell, Book and Candle
Castro Theatre, San Francisco

Tuesday, December 24, 1996
Jerry Maguire
Galaxy Cinema

**Wednesday, December 25,
 1996**
The Whole Wide World
Sunset 5
Lawrence of Arabia
Four Star Theatre

Friday, December 27, 1996
Zentropa and *The Tin Drum*
New Beverly Cinema

Saturday, December 28, 1996
The Crucible
Beverly Center Cinemas

Sunday, December 29, 1996
Dadetown
Nuart

Monday, December 30, 1996
Mother
Beverly Center Cinemas
Casino Royale
New Beverly Cinema

Tuesday, December 31, 1996
Shine
Town Center 5

252

▪ **1997**

Wednesday, January 1, 1997
*Everything You Always
    Wanted to Know About
    Sex . . .* and *Sleeper*
New Beverly Cinema

Thursday, January 2, 1997
The People vs. Larry Flynt
Odeon Broadway (Third Street)

Friday, January 10, 1997
First Strike
Mann's Chinese Theatre

Saturday, January 11, 1997
Turbulence
Galaxy Cinema
The Relic
Mann's Chinese Theatre

Sunday, January 12, 1997
Breaking the Waves
Los Feliz 3
The Night of the Hunter
Tales Café

Friday, January 17, 1997
Citizen Ruth
Fairfax Theatre

Saturday, January 18, 1997
Two for the Road
New Beverly Cinema
The Big Steal
Tales Café
Scream
Galaxy Cinema

Sunday, January 19, 1997
Hamlet (1996)
Royal Theatre, San Francisco

Sunday, January 26, 1997
Betrayed
Tales Café

Friday, January 31, 1997
Evita
Cinerama Dome

Saturday, February 1, 1997
Star Wars (reissue)
Mann's Chinese Theatre

Sunday, February 2, 1997
The Omen
New Beverly Cinema

Monday, February 3, 1997
Angel Face
Tales Café

Friday, February 7, 1997
Night Tide
Raleigh Studios, Chaplin
    Theater

Sunday, February 9, 1997
Where Danger Lives
Tales Café

Monday, February 10, 1997
The Hidden Fortress
New Beverly Cinema

Tuesday, February 11, 1997
Easy Rider
Four Star Theatre
[note: attended AFI Panel
  Discussion]

Saturday, February 15, 1997
Walkabout
Sunset 5

Sunday, February 16, 1997
Ninotchka
Sunset 5
Seconds
New Beverly Cinema

Monday, February 17, 1997
Waiting for Guffman
Nuart

Saturday, February 22, 1997
The Empire Strikes Back
Mann's Chinese Theatre

Sunday, February 23, 1997
Vanishing Point
Four Star Theatre
[note: last screening at the
  Four Star]
[note: 2/27–3/2 attended Aspen
  Comedy Arts Festival]

Saturday, March 1, 1997
This Is Spinal Tap
Stage 3 Theatre, Aspen

Monday, March 3, 1997
The File on Thelma Jordon
Tales Café

Thursday, March 6, 1997
Microcosmos
New Beverly Cinema

Saturday, March 8, 1997
Private Parts
Mann's Chinese Theatre

Sunday, March 9, 1997
Utu
Nuart

Tuesday, March 11, 1997
Donnie Brasco
Beverly Connection Cinema

Thursday, March 13, 1997
The Kingdom
New Beverly Cinema

Saturday, March 15, 1997
Clash by Night
Tales Café

Sunday, March 16, 1997
Modern Romance
New Beverly Cinema

Monday, March 17, 1997
Lost Highway
Sunset 5

Thursday, March 20, 1997
Cat People
Tales Café

Sunday, March 23, 1997
The Godfather
Mann's Chinese Theatre

Wednesday, March 26, 1997
The Curse of the Cat People
Tales Café

Saturday, March 29, 1997
Pickpocket
Grand Illusion Cinema, Seattle
Horror Rises from the Tomb
Sanctuary Theater, Seattle

Sunday, March 30, 1997
Johnny Angel
Tales Café

Tuesday, April 1, 1997
*Monty Python and the Holy
   Grail*
New Beverly Cinema

Wednesday, April 2, 1997
Wise Blood
New Beverly Cinema

Saturday, April 5, 1997
Double Team
Galaxy Cinema

Monday, April 7, 1997
Crash
Sunset 5

Tuesday, April 8, 1997
The Godfather
Mann's Chinese Theatre

Friday, April 11, 1997
Chasing Amy
Sunset 5

Sunday, April 13, 1997
King Kong
Sunset 5

Monday, April 14, 1997
Das Boot
Royal Theatre, San Francisco

Sunday, April 20, 1997
Ride the Pink Horse
Tales Café
Don't Look Now
New Beverly Cinema

Tuesday, April 22, 1997
Anaconda
Galaxy Cinema

Saturday, April 26, 1997
Volcano
Mann's Chinese Theatre

Sunday, April 27, 1997
Grosse Pointe Blank
Mann's Chinese Theatre

Monday, April 28, 1997
Narrow Margin
Tales Café

Thursday, May 1, 1997
The Blade and *Swordsman II*
UCLA James Bridges Theater

Friday, May 2, 1997
Jules and Jim and *The 400
   Blows*
New Beverly Cinema

Saturday, May 3, 1997
The Saint
Beverly Center Cinemas

Thursday, May 8, 1997
The Line-Up
Nuart

Friday, May 9, 1997
Ridicule and *Dangerous*
  Liaisons
New Beverly Cinema

Saturday, May 10, 1997
The Fifth Element
Cinerama Dome

Sunday, May 11, 1997
Where's Poppa?
New Beverly Cinema

Monday, May 12, 1997
The Desperate Hours
Tales Café
Austin Powers
Los Feliz 3

Tuesday, May 13, 1997
Shaft
Nuart

Wednesday, May 14, 1997
Night Moves
Nuart

Saturday, May 17, 1997
When We Were Kings
Monica 4-Plex

Sunday, May 18, 1997
Westworld and *Rollerball*
New Beverly Cinema

Monday, May 19, 1997
Night of the Living Dead
Tales Café

Wednesday, May 21, 1997
The Crimson Kimono
New Beverly Cinema

Thursday, May 22, 1997
Underworld U.S.A.
New Beverly Cinema

Friday, May 23, 1997
Judex
Raleigh Studios, Chaplin
  Theater

Saturday, May 24, 1997
The Lost World
Galaxy Cinema
Breathless
New Beverly Cinema

Sunday, May 25, 1997
Fetishes
Sunset 5

Monday, May 26, 1997
Naked Alibi
Tales Café

Saturday, May 31, 1997
Shadowman
Raleigh Studios, Chaplin
  Theater

Saturday, June 7, 1997
Con Air
Regency II

Monday, June 9, 1997
Crime by Night
Tales Café

Tuesday, June 10, 1997
The Island of Dr. Moreau
Mann's Chinese Theatre

Wednesday, June 11, 1997
Pather Panchali
New Beverly Cinema

Sunday, June 15, 1997
The Long Goodbye
New Beverly Cinema

Tuesday, June 17, 1997
White Zombie
Tales Café

Saturday, June 21, 1997
Batman and Robin
Mann's Chinese Theatre

Sunday, June 22, 1997
Thieves' Highway
Tales Café

Monday, June 23, 1997
The Pink Panther
New Beverly Cinema

Tuesday, June 24, 1997
*Battles Without Honour and
    Humanity*
DGA Theater

Thursday, June 26, 1997
The Professionals
Monica 4-Plex

Sunday, June 29, 1997
Face/Off
Mann's Chinese Theatre

Monday, June 30, 1997
T-Men
Tales Café

Wednesday, July 2, 1997
Men in Black
Cinerama Dome

Friday, July 4, 1997
Contempt
Nuart
*Life and Opinion of Masseur
    Ichi*
Raleigh Studios, Chaplin
    Theater

Saturday, July 5, 1997
Rio Bravo
Monica 4-Plex
This Gun for Hire
Tales Café

Thursday, July 10, 1997
Ocean's Eleven
Raleigh Studios, Chaplin
    Theater

FOUR YEARS OF FILMS

Saturday, July 12, 1997
Five Easy Pieces and *The Last Picture Show*
New Beverly Cinema

Thursday, July 17, 1997
Stray Dog
Tales Café

Friday, July 18, 1997
Operation Condor
Galaxy Cinema

Saturday, July 19, 1997
The Three Stooges Meet Hercules
Nuart (midnight show)

Sunday, July 20, 1997
The Fearless Vampire Killers
New Beverly Cinema

Monday, July 28, 1997
The President's Analyst
Tales Café

Tuesday, July 29, 1997
Dog Day Afternoon and *Serpico*
New Beverly Cinema

Wednesday, July 30, 1997
The Wrong Guy
DGA Theater

Thursday, July 31, 1997
Nostalghia
New Beverly Cinema

Saturday, August 2, 1997
Forty Guns, I Shot Jesse James and *The Baron of Arizona*
Raleigh Studios, Chaplin Theater

Sunday, August 3, 1997
In the Company of Men
Sunset 5

Thursday, August 7, 1997
Air Force One
Galaxy Cinema

Sunday, August 10, 1997
Cape Fear
Kennedy Center/AFI Silver Theater

Monday, August 11, 1997
It's a Wonderful Life
Nuart

Saturday, August 16, 1997
Somewhere in the Night
Tales Café

Wednesday, August 20, 1997
Carrie
New Beverly Cinema

Monday, August 25, 1997
The Uninvited
Tales Café

258

FOUR YEARS OF FILMS

Thursday, August 28, 1997
The Silencers and *Our Man Flint*
Raleigh Studios, Chaplin Theater

Sunday, August 31, 1997
Grey Gardens and *Salesman*
Grand Illusion Cinema, Seattle

Wednesday, September 3, 1997
Cul-de-sac
New Beverly Cinema

Monday, September 8, 1997
Moonrise
Tales Café

Tuesday, September 9, 1997
Woman in the Dunes
Nuart

Sunday, September 14, 1997
The 7th Voyage of Sinbad
New Beverly Cinema

Monday, September 15, 1997
Jason and the Argonauts
New Beverly Cinema

Sunday, September 21, 1997
Thunder Road and *The Friends of Eddie Coyle*
New Beverly Cinema

Monday, September 29, 1997
Band of Outsiders
Tales Café

Tuesday, September 30, 1997
Dial M for Murder
New Beverly Cinema

Friday, October 3, 1997
L.A. Confidential
Mann's Chinese Theatre

Sunday, October 5, 1997
Fast, Cheap and Out of Control
Nuart
A Funny Thing Happened on the Way to the Forum
New Beverly Cinema

Wednesday, October 8, 1997
Visions of Light
New Beverly Cinema
The Full Monty
Los Feliz 3

Friday, October 10, 1997
Niagara
Tales Café
Alphaville
New Beverly Cinema

Saturday, October 11, 1997
Long Day's Journey into Night and *Tabu*
UCLA Melnitz

Monday, October 13, 1997
Evil Dead II: Dead by Dawn
Mann Plaza Theatre

Wednesday, October 15, 1997
Shock Corridor
Roxie Theater, San Francisco

FOUR YEARS OF FILMS

Saturday, October 18, 1997
Shall We Dance?
Bridge Theater, San Francisco

Sunday, October 19, 1997
The Game
Kabuki 8, San Francisco

Monday, October 20, 1997
I Walked with a Zombie
Tales Café

Wednesday, October 22, 1997
Mad Love and *The Devil-Doll*
Warner Grand Theatre, San
    Pedro

Thursday, October 23, 1997
Blow-Up
New Beverly Cinema

Friday, October 24, 1997
The Philadelphia Story
New Beverly Cinema

Sunday, October 26, 1997
Leopard Man
Tales Café
A Better Tomorrow
New Beverly Cinema

Monday, October 27, 1997
The Devil's Advocate
Mann's Chinese Theatre

Wednesday, October 29, 1997
Eraserhead and *The Elephant
    Man*
New Beverly Cinema

Thursday, October 30, 1997
Boogie Nights
Galaxy Cinema

Friday, October 31, 1997
The Masque of the Red Death
    and *House of Usher*
Cinerama Dome

Saturday, November 1, 1997
*Plan 9 from Outer Space, I
    Married a Monster from
    Outer Space, The Tingler,
    Mr. Sardonicus* and
    Daughter of Horror
Cinerama Dome

Sunday, November 2, 1997
Ministry of Fear
Castro Theatre, San Francisco

Wednesday, November 5, 1997
To Have and Have Not
Warner Grand Theatre, San
    Pedro

Saturday, November 8, 1997
Starship Troopers
Cinerama Dome
Bean
Mann's Chinese Theatre

Tuesday, November 11, 1997
The Haunting
LACMA
Cronos
New Beverly Cinema

Saturday, November 15, 1997
Seven Beauties
Raleigh Studios, Chaplin
  Theater

Sunday, November 16, 1997
Super Fly and *The Mack*
New Beverly Cinema

**Wednesday, November 19,
  1997**
Jailhouse Rock and *Viva Las
  Vegas*
Warner Grand Theatre, San
  Pedro

Thursday, November 20, 1997
The Locket
Tales Café
*The Man Who Knew Too
  Much*
New Beverly Cinema

Friday, November 21, 1997
*Sick: The Life & Death of Bob
  Flanagan, Supermasochist*
Los Feliz 3
*Midnight in the Garden of
  Good and Evil*
Mann's Chinese Theatre

Saturday, November 22, 1997
Swept Away
Raleigh Studios, Chaplin
  Theater

Sunday, November 23, 1997
The Trip and *Head*
New Beverly Cinema

**Wednesday, November 26,
  1997**
Alien: Resurrection
Mann's Chinese Theatre

Friday, November 28, 1997
The Ice Storm
Los Feliz 3

Saturday, November 29, 1997
The Sweet Hereafter
Sunset 5

Sunday, November 30, 1997
The Artist's Revolution
Sunset 5

Friday, December 5, 1997
Scream 2
Galaxy Cinema

Monday, December 8, 1997
Cry Danger
Tales Café

Sunday, December 14, 1997
Deconstructing Harry
Showcase

Monday, December 15, 1997
And Then There Were None
Tales Café

**Wednesday, December 17,
  1997**
Sweet Smell of Success
New Beverly Cinema

Friday, December 19, 1997
Tomorrow Never Dies
Galaxy Cinema

Thursday, December 25, 1997
As Good as It Gets
Los Feliz 3

Saturday, December 27, 1997
White Heat
Roxie Theater, San Francisco

Sunday, December 28, 1997
The Letter
Roxie Theater, San Francisco

■ **1998**

Thursday, January 1, 1998
What Ever Happened to Baby Jane?
New Beverly Cinema

Friday, January 16, 1998
Wag the Dog
Los Feliz 3

Sunday, January 18, 1998
One False Move
New Beverly Cinema

Monday, January 19, 1998
Reform School Girl
Tales Café

Tuesday, January 20, 1998
Hard Rain
Galaxy Cinema

Wednesday, January 21, 1998
Good Will Hunting
Galaxy Cinema

Sunday, January 25, 1998
Spice World
Cineplex Odeon, Seattle

Sunday, February 1, 1998
Gonin
Nuart

Monday, February 2, 1998
The Apostle
Sunset 5

Tuesday, February 3, 1998
Titanic
Mann's Chinese Theatre

Friday, February 6, 1998
The Replacement Killers
Cinerama Dome

Saturday, February 7, 1998
World for Ransom
Raleigh Studios

Monday, February 9, 1998
Outside the Wall
Tales Café

Tuesday, February 10, 1998
West Side Story
New Beverly Cinema

Saturday, February 14, 1998
Withnail & I
New Beverly Cinema
The Wedding Singer
Beverly Center Cinemas

Sunday, February 15, 1998
Experiment in Terror and *In Cold Blood*
New Beverly Cinema

Wednesday, February 18, 1998
Double Agent 73 and *Bad Girls Go to Hell*
Nuart

Thursday, February 19, 1998
Let Me Die a Woman
Nuart

Friday, February 20, 1998
The Legend of Lylah Clare
Raleigh Studios

Saturday, February 21, 1998
Network and *The Conversation*
New Beverly Cinema

Sunday, March 1, 1998
Dark City
Varsity Cinema, Toronto

Monday, March 2, 1998
Children of Paradise
New Beverly Cinema

Wednesday, March 4, 1998
Coffy
Mission Street Theater-Pub, Portland, Oregon

Thursday, March 5, 1998
Jackie Brown
Mission Street Theater-Pub, Portland, Oregon

Friday, March 6, 1998
The Big Lebowski
Sherman Oaks Galleria

Monday, March 9, 1998
Hidden Fear
Tales Café

Saturday, March 14, 1998
Waco: The Rules of Engagement
Sunset 5
Mean Streets
Nuart

Sunday, March 15, 1998
Room Service
New Beverly Cinema
Men with Guns
Sunset 5

Tuesday, March 17, 1998
A Night at the Opera
New Beverly Cinema

Wednesday, March 18, 1998
Thelonious Monk: Straight, No Chaser
New Beverly Cinema

FOUR YEARS OF FILMS

Thursday, March 19, 1998
Let's Get Lost
New Beverly Cinema

Friday, March 20, 1998
Mr. Nice Guy
Cinerama Dome
Wild Things
Galaxy Cinema

Saturday, March 21, 1998
The Producers and *It's a Mad,*
Mad, Mad, Mad World
New Beverly Cinema

Saturday, March 28, 1998
James Ellroy: Demon Dog of
American Crime Fiction
Nuart

Monday, April 6, 1998
42nd Street
Mann's Chinese Theatre

Tuesday, April 7, 1998
Now, Voyager
Mann's Chinese Theatre
The Naked Kiss
Nuart

Wednesday, April 8, 1998
The Searchers
Mann's Chinese Theatre

Thursday, April 9, 1998
Days of Wine and Roses
Castro Theatre

Tuesday, April 14, 1998
Spike and Mike's Festival of
Animation
Castro Theatre

Thursday, April 16, 1998
Underground
New Beverly Cinema

Friday, April 17, 1998
Kurt and Courtney
Sunset 5
Winchester '73, *T-Men* and
Desperate
Raleigh Studios, Chaplin
Theater

Saturday, April 18, 1998
Z
New Beverly Cinema
The Naked Spur, *Raw Deal*
and *Railroaded*
Raleigh Studios, Chaplin
Theater

Sunday, April 19, 1998
The Big Knife
New Beverly Cinema

Monday, April 20, 1998
The Spanish Prisoner
Royal Theatre, San Francisco

Wednesday, April 22, 1998
The Big One
Sunset 5

FOUR YEARS OF FILMS

Friday, April 24, 1998
Bend of the River and *Border
    Incident*
Raleigh Studios, Chaplin
    Theater

Sunday, April 26, 1998
The Big Hit
Beverly Connection Cinema

Wednesday, April 29, 1998
Wild Man Blues
Nuart

Saturday, May 2, 1998
*Three Wise Girls, Man's
    Castle* and *Love Affair*
Nuart

Sunday, May 3, 1998
*Ann Carver's Profession, Black
    Moon* and *The Man I Stole*
Nuart

Tuesday, May 5, 1998
Tomorrow Never Dies
Galaxy Cinema

Wednesday, May 6, 1998
Behind the Mask
Nuart

Friday, May 8, 1998
The Kingdom II
Nuart

Saturday, May 9, 1998
Black Dog
Galaxy Cinema

Friday, May 15, 1998
Shoot the Piano Player
Tales Café

Saturday, May 16, 1998
Body Heat and *The Postman
    Always Rings Twice*
New Beverly Cinema
Deep Impact
Beverly Connection Cinema

Sunday, May 17, 1998
Logan's Run
New Beverly Cinema

Tuesday, May 19, 1998
Jour de Fête
Nuart

Friday, May 22, 1998
Enter the Dragon
Nuart

Saturday, May 23, 1998
Godzilla
Cinerama Dome

Sunday, May 24, 1998
*Fear and Loathing in Las
    Vegas*
Galaxy Cinema

Monday, May 25, 1998
Cabaret and *New York, New
    York*
New Beverly Cinema

FOUR YEARS OF FILMS

Sunday, May 31, 1998
The Terminator
New Beverly Cinema

Monday, June 1, 1998
Second Breath
Tales Café

Friday, June 5, 1998
The Truman Show
Mann's Chinese Theatre

Saturday, June 6, 1998
Bulworth
Los Feliz 3

Monday, June 8, 1998
Duck Soup
New Beverly Cinema

Thursday, June 11, 1998
The Opposite of Sex
Los Feliz 3

Friday, June 12, 1998
Dirty Work
Galaxy Cinema

Saturday, June 13, 1998
Le Trou
Raleigh Studios, Chaplin
    Theater

Sunday, June 14, 1998
Forbidden Planet and *The
    Time Machine*
New Beverly Cinema

Thursday, June 18, 1998
Don't Look Back
Nuart

Friday, June 19, 1998
The X-Files
Mann's Chinese Theatre

Monday, June 22, 1998
The House on 92nd Street
Tales Café

Wednesday, June 24, 1998
The Tenth Victim
Nuart

Sunday, June 28, 1998
Destroy All Monsters
Nuart

Tuesday, June 30, 1998
Dersu Uzala
New Beverly Cinema

Wednesday, July 1, 1998
Armageddon
Galaxy Cinema
Picnic at Hanging Rock
Nuart

Friday, July 3, 1998
Hail, Mafia!
Raleigh Studios, Chaplin
    Theater

Sunday, July 5, 1998
*Godzilla vs. the Smog
    Monster*
Nuart

Monday, July 6, 1998
High Art
Sunset 5

Friday, July 10, 1998
Small Soldiers
Beverly Center Cinemas

Saturday, July 11, 1998
Série Noire
Raleigh Studios, Chaplin
 Theater

Sunday, July 12, 1998
*Ghidra, the Three-Headed
 Monster*
Nuart

Sunday, July 19, 1998
99.9
Cinéma Impérial, Montreal

Monday, July 20, 1998
Stardust Memories
Pre Cinema

Thursday, July 30, 1998
The Negotiator
Galaxy Cinema
Naked Lunch
New Beverly Cinema

Saturday, August 1, 1998
*There's Something About
 Mary*
Los Feliz 3

Saturday, August 8, 1998
Snake Eyes
Mann's Chinese Theatre
Bigger Than Life
Raleigh Studios, Chaplin
 Theater

Sunday, August 9, 1998
Halloween: H20
Galaxy Cinema
Saving Private Ryan
Mann's Chinese Theatre

Friday, August 14, 1998
Crimewave
Raleigh Studios

Sunday, August 16, 1998
Grey Gardens
Nuart

Saturday, August 22, 1998
It's a Gift
Old Town Music Hall
The Sword of Doom and
 Cemetery Without Crosses
Raleigh Studios, Chaplin
 Theater

Sunday, August 23, 1998
Blade
Galaxy Cinema

Tuesday, September 1, 1998
Excalibur
New Beverly Cinema

Thursday, September 3, 1998
L'Avventura
New Beverly Cinema

Saturday, September 12, 1998
Touch of Evil
Nuart

Sunday, September 13, 1998
Some Like It Hot
New Beverly Cinema

Tuesday, September 15, 1998
Your Friends and Neighbors
Dream Theater

Friday, September 18, 1998
Rush Hour
Mann's Chinese Theatre

Wednesday, September 23, 1998
Sid and Nancy
New Beverly Cinema

Friday, September 25, 1998
Charles Mingus: Triumph of the Underdog, Dexter Gordon: More Than You Know and *Art Pepper: Notes from a Jazz Survivor*
LACMA, Leo S. Bing Theater

Monday, September 28, 1998
Permanent Midnight
Sunset 5

Thursday, October 1, 1998
The Glass Web
Tales Café

Sunday, October 4, 1998
Bring Me the Head of Alfredo Garcia and *The Wild Bunch*
New Beverly Cinema

Tuesday, October 6, 1998
Day for Night
Royal Theatre

Sunday, October 11, 1998
Fantastic Planet
Nuart

Monday, October 12, 1998
Love Is the Devil
Sunset 5

Saturday, October 17, 1998
See the Sea (w/ A Summer Dress)
Sunset 5
Happiness
Sunset 5

Sunday, October 18, 1998
All That Jazz
Sunset 5

Monday, October 19, 1998
The Old Dark House
Grand Illusion Cinema

FOUR YEARS OF FILMS

Tuesday, October 27, 1998
Pleasantville
Galaxy Cinema

Friday, October 30, 1998
Mystery of the Wax Museum
   and *The Shining*
Orpheum Theatre

Saturday, October 31, 1998
Them!
Orpheum Theatre

Sunday, November 1, 1998
The Lady Eve
New Beverly Cinema

Wednesday, November 4, 1998
Persona
New Beverly Cinema

Thursday, November 12, 1998
The Cruise
Nuart

Friday, November 13, 1998
Background to Danger
Tales Café

Saturday, November 14, 1998
Gods and Monsters
Sunset 5

Sunday, November 22, 1998
Modern Times and *City*
   Lights
New Beverly Cinema
The Cruise
Music Hall

Friday, November 27, 1998
Elizabeth
Vista Theatre

Sunday, November 29, 1998
Thunderball and *On Her*
   Majesty's Secret Service
New Beverly Cinema

Sunday, December 6, 1998
The Ten Commandments
Egyptian Theatre

Monday, December 7, 1998
Dracula's Daughter
Nuart

Friday, December 11, 1998
Star Trek: Insurrection
El Portal Theatre

Monday, December 14, 1998
Abbott and Costello Meet
   Frankenstein and *The*
   Invisible Man
Nuart

Tuesday, December 15, 1998
Murders in the Rue
   Morgue and *House of*
   Frankenstein
Nuart

Wednesday, December 16,
   1998
Viridiana and *The*
   Exterminating Angel
New Beverly Cinema

FOUR YEARS OF FILMS

Sunday, December 20, 1998
A Simple Plan
Vista Theatre

Tuesday, December 22, 1998
The Thin Red Line
Samuel Goldwyn Theater

Wednesday, December 23, 1998
Touch of Evil and *The Lady from Shanghai*
New Beverly Cinema

Friday, December 25, 1998
Patch Adams
Galaxy Cinema
Hurlyburly
Sunset 5

Saturday, December 26, 1998
Shakespeare in Love
Los Feliz 3

Sunday, December 27, 1998
The General
Sunset 5

Monday, December 28, 1998
The Man Who Fell to Earth
New Beverly Cinema

Wednesday, December 30, 1998
Sisters
New Beverly Cinema

▪ 1999

Friday, January 1, 1999
The Celebration
Los Feliz 3

Sunday, January 17, 1999
Nashville
New Beverly Cinema

Friday, January 22, 1999
A Merry War
New Beverly Cinema
Life Is Beautiful
Cecchi Gori Fine Arts Theatre

Saturday, January 23, 1999
A Civil Action
El Capitan Theatre

Sunday, January 24, 1999
Still Crazy
Showcase

Thursday, February 4, 1999
What's the Matter with Helen? and *The Killing Kind*
Nuart

Saturday, February 6, 1999
Rushmore
Sunset 5

Sunday, February 7, 1999
Blade Runner
Cinerama Dome

Tuesday, February 16, 1999
Rushmore
Sunset 5
Mr. Smith Goes to Washington and *It Happened One Night*
Cinerama Dome

Wednesday, February 17, 1999
The Virgin Spring
New Beverly Cinema

Friday, February 19, 1999
Jawbreaker
Galaxy Cinema

Sunday, February 21, 1999
Man of the West
New Beverly Cinema

Tuesday, February 23, 1999
On the Waterfront and *From Here to Eternity*
Cinerama Dome

Friday, February 26, 1999
Weekend
New Beverly Cinema

Wednesday, March 17, 1999
The Brandon Teena Story
Nuart

Wednesday, March 24, 1999
Shadow of a Doubt
Castro Theatre, San Francisco

Thursday, March 25, 1999
Lenny Bruce: Swear to Tell the Truth
Roxie Theater, San Francisco

Saturday, March 27, 1999
Ravenous
Regency II

Wednesday, March 31, 1999
The Reckless Moment
New Beverly Cinema

Friday, April 2, 1999
Brazil
Nuart
Armored Car Robbery
Egyptian Theatre

Saturday, April 3, 1999
The Killer That Stalked New York and *99 River Street*
Egyptian Theatre

Sunday, April 4, 1999
Mad Max and *Death Race 2000*
New Beverly Cinema

Thursday, April 8, 1999
High and Low and *Ikiru*
New Beverly Cinema

Friday, April 9, 1999
Go
Los Feliz 3

FOUR YEARS OF FILMS

Saturday, April 10, 1999
Sullivan's Travels and *The
    Miracle of Morgan's Creek*
New Beverly Cinema

Sunday, April 11, 1999
Nightmare Alley
Egyptian Theatre

Friday, April 16, 1999
The Matrix
Mann's Chinese Theatre

Sunday, April 18, 1999
Aguirre, the Wrath of God
New Beverly

Friday, April 23, 1999
The Birds and *The Trouble
    with Harry*
Nuart

Sunday, April 25, 1999
Burden of Dreams (w/ *Werner
    Herzog Eats His Shoe*)
Grand Illusion Cinema, Seattle

Wednesday, April 28, 1999
Torn Curtain
Nuart

Friday, April 30, 1999
Marnie
Nuart

Thursday, May 6, 1999
The Blair Witch Project
    [video]

Friday, May 7, 1999
Election
Showcase

Saturday, May 8, 1999
The Mummy
Galaxy Cinema

Thursday, May 20, 1999
*Star Wars Episode I: The
    Phantom Menace*
Vista Theatre